BODY TYPES

BODY TYPES

JOEL FRIEDLANDER

1986

GLOBE PRESS BOOKS

NEW YORK

Composed in ITC New Baskerville by U.S. Lithograph
and Globe Press Books, New York City.
Printed and bound by McNaughton & Gunn,
Ann Arbor, Michigan.

ISBN: 0-936385-18-9 Clothbound
        0-936385-17-0 Paperbound

Library of Congress Catalog Card No.: 86-82344

10   9   8   7   6   5   4   3   2
MANUFACTURED IN THE UNITED STATES.

CONTENTS

MEN

AND TYPES

JILL, MY WIFE, AND I ARE SITTING at home listening to a friend of ours:

"Doesn't this putting people into pigeonholes," he says, "really determine what you're going to see in them? I mean, it's like astrology, isn't it? It's okay by itself, but as soon as you take it into a different context, it doesn't seem to have any relevance at all. Am I right?"

You understand, I'm watching this fellow, and while he's talking I'm thinking about him: his shaved head looks like a fireplug; his hands chop aggressively at the air while he's speaking; he's got a feisty build, barrel-chested and bandy-legged; and when he's relaxed, as he is now, a commanding air settles over him. Then he starts to look a little like a general from an antique empire, Marcus Lucillus Somebody, contemplating the most efficient way to ram civilization down the beastly throats of the local barbarians. It may not be an agreeable job, but it's one that's got to be done, and it's his.

This surging *Martial* atmosphere makes sense to me, because I've seen it before, but it's difficult to explain to my friend—as difficult as it would be to make him hear the Martial drum beat that seems to mark the cadence of his march as he paces up the room, and down.

Here's a man who dresses in a military fashion, although his most aggressive instincts have for some time been channeled into peaceful ventures. He roams the world alone, armed with the equipment he thinks will prepare him for any situation that may crop up. He's frank, and thinks people should say what they feel; his books are full of this frankness and brimming with his advice to take life by the horns, wrestle it, suffer it, defeat it. When he takes up a cause it becomes a holy crusade, to be carried on at volume.

Enough. Sure, my friend also has a gentler side to his nature that, if added, would certainly color the picture I'm painting. It is a picture of a man, and also of his body type. Certainly he's a distinct and exhilarating person; that's what we prize him for. He's also a Martial type. The path of his rush through life follows the track of his own private war from battlefield to battlefield.

The name I'm using for this group of characteristics is Mars, but it could as easily be another: adrenal; arian, after Ares; warrior; pioneer; soldier. To me it represents the planet Mars, the ancient god Mars that exemplified these traits, and the body type that is their namesake.

I know that this friend of ours, and the other people to whom I've mentioned this idea, think it odd. It either offends them, or seems irrelevant. They don't see how they might apply it, they doubt that it's true, and they maintain that even if it were true, surely they would have noticed it long ago.

To be able to see that people are types is a remarkable, even shattering, experience. People are quite right to think it strange that something this obvious should have escaped them, but it has. It's as strange as never having noticed the color of your own hair, how tall your wife is, or something equally absurd.

Yet we all have a feel for types; we know the kind of person we're attracted to, for instance, and the ones that always rub us the wrong way. It just never occurred to us to look deeper into these feelings, or to see whether there was more meaning in them.

It's difficult to admit that we could know types if we were told about them. We won't believe it. If we're presented with a systematic explanation for our sense of types, and shown what types look like and how to find them, we're skeptical. Even if it's explained to us that we could see people's types, and by doing so revolutionize our understanding of men, the whole idea seems unbelievable, it seems repugnant, or it seems simply impossible.

* * *

Of course, the notion that people are types, that they can be classified according to some fixed set of traits, is hardly a new idea; it's one of the most ancient. It's an idea that punctuates the early history of science, finds a place in the teachings of many primitive religions, and has been forgotten, overlooked, or debunked more times, in more places, by more people, than we can count.

Although it seems to us something of a dream, thinking of people as specific types has never really died out; it still has a hold on our imagination, and continues to be fashionable today. Looking at some of the ways in which the idea of types has existed before, how it was formulated, and how it was practiced, may demonstrate that the idea of types isn't so strange after all; we've just stopped taking it as seriously as people once did.

First, and by far the most familiar of these ways of classifying people, is astrology. Who hasn't been fascinated by the possibilities that seem to lurk in his own astrological type—his sign—and in the information that's supposed to come along with it? Who hasn't wondered whether there are truly insights to be gained from astrology's systemic definition of people?

I know I have. And almost everybody I meet must have an interest as well, because it's hard to come across someone who doesn't know his sign and a little bit about what it's supposed to say about him. We've all been introduced to the person who opens his presentation with an astrological aside, "I'm a Capricorn". He's pleased his new boss is a Gemini; he's always got along with Geminis in the past.

These common situations acknowledge, however unconsciously, the existence of types. While we may not delve any further into astrology than an occasional glance at the newspaper, (that superstitious searching for the omen of the day), neither do we forget our sign, nor completely lose the vestiges of our identification with it.

Then there are those cultures whose members believe in types implicitly; the whole social structure is built around the idea. In these cultures the population is confined within the strict boundaries of *caste*—a hereditary ranking that divides people by rigid lines and restricts the jobs they can hold, whom they can marry, even where they can live.

In such a society you're a priest or a servant, married or not, live in poverty or splendor, depending on your position in the hierarchy; that is, according to your inherited type. While these hereditary divisions are applied to vast groups of people rather than to individuals, they reinforce the idea of types just as strongly as any other method of classification.

For a society grounded on caste, the best model we have today is that of Hindu India. Thousands of separate castes, *jatis*, embody people's religious customs, their occupations, and their cultural status. Four hereditary social classes further divide the populace; *Brahmans*, who become priests and scholars; *Kshatriyas*, who populate the military and contribute the rulers of the country; *Vaisyas*, who work the fields and mind the shops; *Sudras*, common peasants and laborers. Added to these are the untouchables, standing somewhat outside the caste system, who have for centuries been relegated to the most menial chores.

Untouchability, in fact, has been outlawed by pro-

11

gressive governments in India since 1949. But despite this legislation, and despite the pressures of our democratic age which are slowly eroding at least the occupational barriers, these social distinctions remain strong and resist change. They survive because they're rooted in the entrenched attitudes of a long cultural history. Although caste seems an anachronism to us today, there have been many more examples of its highly structured organization in the past.

We can look to the ancient gods of Greece for another example of the historical existence of types. The Greeks of classical antiquity saw their gods not just as deities, but as representatives of their own inner drives—those universal forces that move us all, like passion, anger, love, patriotism, or jealousy. The influence of the gods was exactly the influence of one or another of these drives, and the struggles amongst the gods, told and retold in legend and song, were also reflections of man's inner conflicts.

Apollo and Dionysus make a good example. Apollo exemplified order and reason; he was at odds with Dionysus, the proponent of sensuality and license. But each of us is split along these lines, our own cool reason contending with our impulse to let go, to indulge all our appetites to their maximum.

What the Greeks valued most of all was a harmony that could be achieved through a balance of these forces, a harmony created when both logic and license played their part, and in which neither completely dominated. When Apollo reigns, it is reason that rules our

12

actions; Dionysus makes us long for relaxation and release, for forgetting the duties that confine us. A man who is chiefly swayed by one or the other, who always follows either reason or release, could be assigned all the attributes of that god. Apollo or Dionysus would rule him, and determine what type of man he is.

Seven of these gods became associated with the seven visible heavenly bodies, and their qualities have been bound together ever since. These connections have lasted through more than two thousand years, and find a place in our time in the names we use for the planets and the days of the week. Each day has its god, and we have no difficulty in considering the whole week as a complete and self-contained system.

Monday belongs to the moon, ruled by Selene; Tuesday is Mars' day, under Ares; Mercury presides over Wednesday, the day of Hermes; Thursday belongs to Jupiter, whose god is Zeus; Friday is Venus' day, ruled by Aphrodite; Saturday is Saturn-day, the old Greek Kronos; and Sunday is the day of the Sun, ruled not by Apollo, but by Phoebus. Although we use these names every day, we've forgotten their ancient origins. The beliefs that built this system have lost their power, and no longer move us.

About twelve hundred years closer to home, during the gothic era, the idea of types appears again—as one element in the symbolism invented by the builders of the great cathedrals. I'm referring particularly to twenty-eight figures that once ranged across the face of the

Cathedral of Notre Dame in Paris, presumably sculptures of ancient kings.

But there's also a tradition that these figures represented body types, were meant to demonstrate a knowledge of types, and were intended to instruct an illiterate populace in this knowledge through visible examples. The twenty-eight are the result of seven basic types multiplied by the four kinds of dispositions each type might have.

Some of these statues, "lost" during the destruction that accompanied the French Revolution, have recently been unearthed and put on display. I saw them in New York, when they were displayed briefly a few years ago, and also at the Cluny Museum in Paris, their permanent home. I was unable to tell whether they are in fact, meant to represent types, but several of these grave, intent faces emanate a force that's in all really transcendental art; they hint at universal laws.

The idea of types surfaces again in the middle ages, when it was championed by the alchemists—the mystic chemists of that time. Besides pioneering the systematic study of chemistry, they also devised a scheme of human types. It was built, as so many others have been, on the planetary model.

The alchemists wanted to fix the actions and interactions of metals that were important to their experiments in transmutation; they thought each of these metals was ruled by one of the seven visible planets. But these alchemists, using the same information, classified people as well. They decided that each man had a preponderance of one of the basic metals, and that this preponderance determined, among other things, a man's temperament, his physique, and his susceptibility to specific illnesses.

It's melancholy to consider the medieval alchemists today. Their experiments, based on unprovable theories, couldn't withstand the pressure of constant failure. The alchemists were incapable of producing the gold their theories predicted they would. Yet it was an enlightened philosophy that led them to pursue their strange science, a philosophy intimately bound up with mysticism and the quest for human perfection.

The alchemists with the most profound aspirations weren't trying to amass personal wealth. They were trying to prove that the laws which ruled their philosophy could be applied to every level of existence, the material world as well as the spiritual; that they were objective laws.

There's no lack of types in literature, where we expect to find them. After all, much of the pleasure and a good deal of the insight we get from literature come from our ability to see a character struggling within the confines of his typical behavior. We appreciate these symbolic characters especially when they remind us of people we know—they come to represent their type in our thinking. Literary characters often become archetypes for whole classes of people, and enable us to objectify, and to explain, their behavior.

Shakespeare's *Othello* rings with this use of character, although body types only provide the stage on which he built this remarkable play. Othello, the Moor, is courageous, impetuous, and passionate; he's a picture of Mars, on whose behalf he wages the wars of state. Iago operates by deceit, treachery, and calculation, lying easily whenever it's necessary to further his diabolical ends; he's a caricature of all the worst sides of Mercury. The action of the play as it descends to its inevitable and murderous conclusion springs largely from the instinctive antagonism of these two types.

Characters like Othello and Iago, locked together in their tragic destiny for all time, never change. As individuals they're incapable of change precisely because they're unable to alter a course once they've embarked on it. I've watched them play out this dance of death over and over, as others have for hundreds of years, and it never fails to touch me. Shakespeare has stretched the impulses in their types almost to the point of caricature. They've passed beyond simple examples of their types, and gone on to become bloody exaggerations of their most murderous features. In every performance their involuntary behavior fires the unreasoned hatred in their types, and defeats them.

The advent of "scientific psychology" has seen the idea of body types decline in importance; it's treated as "unscientific." One of the few exceptions to this trend was an American anthropologist, William Sheldon. Having photographed thousands of subjects, Sheldon arrived at a method of dividing people into three types. He attempted to link three distinct kinds of temperaments to the three types of bodies in his scheme. These divisions were based on his theory that each type had developed from a different layer of cells in the embryo, and he named them after these three cellular levels; ectomorph, mesomorph, and endomorph.

Sheldon's ectomorph grew from the ectoderm, the outer layer of cells in the embryo, from which also grow the skin, hair, nails and the nervous system. These ectomorphs were wiry, and had a surplus of nervous energy. His mesomorph grew from the middle layer of cells, which also gives rise to the skeletal, muscular, and connective tissue as well as the circulatory, excretory, and reproductive systems. Mesomorphs had a muscular, sturdy build. Endomorphs were reputed to grow from the innermost cell layer, from which the digestive glands, the lining of the alimentary tract, and the lungs also grew. Endomorphs are the heavyweights among us.

This scheme, which received widespread publicity, remains popular today. Its attraction has a good deal to do with its simplicity. And while it could have provided the impetus for further research into the idea that psychological traits might correspond to the build of the body, instead it has lingered on the fringes of academic respectability. However, researchers in another discipline have attacked the same problem, and we can look to the fruits of their investigations for information that is decisive to the theory of types.

Endocrinology, which studies the glands that regulate many of the body's systems through hormones, has produced a different method for typing people. Dr.

Louis Berman delved into this idea, and assembled an entire plan of types built on glandular imbalances.

Berman thought that the over-activity of each gland produced a type that bore all the markings of that gland's functions. He even looked back through history for examples, and included in his books illustrations for each of these types. His descriptions included not only the appearance of each type, but the results of their particular glandular imbalance on their personality. For instance, his adrenal type usually had bright red hair, freckles, and an explosive disposition.

Unfortunately, Dr. Berman's theories have been neglected even more than Sheldon's have, and are almost unknown today. Perhaps it's been the rise of democratic thinking, with its insistence that "all men are created equal," that's closed the door on the study of human types. It goes against the grain of our education. We can't imagine a typology that isn't bigotry, or worse. Now the idea of types is in ill-repute, scorned as quackery or feared as prejudice, and these attitudes shut us off from any real study of body types.

*   *   *

Several of the systems of classifying people that I've mentioned grew from common roots, even though they flowered in different ways. They were schemes originally conceived, interpreted, and transmitted by unusual teachers in unusual schools, all of whom were connected in one way or another with the practice of

18

mysticism. Among the astrologers and astronomers, the builders of the gothic cathedrals, and the alchemists were some who focussed all their energy on inner understanding, searching for the knowledge that would lead them to a personal, mystical revelation. The idea of body types would have occupied a significant spot in their interest.

However, the little knowledge that remains from these schools describes the types in arcane, symbolic, or forgotten languages; it doesn't tell us how to observe them ourselves. It's possible that the methods invented for applying the knowledge of types were kept on the hidden, esoteric side of these teachings. They may never have carried farther than the sound of a teacher's voice. Since these methods would invariably have been designed for the people of a specific time in a specific culture, they wouldn't have lived nearly as long as the philosophy that produced them. In any event, someone looking for a way to make use of this knowledge would have found, until recently, very little to help them.

I suppose it was natural, if not inevitable, that when the idea of body types appeared again it would be as part of a system of thought linked to practical mysticism. This time, it surfaced within the stream of events that carried an Armenian-Greek from Southern Russia off to Asia in search of hidden knowledge. It was a stream that eventually swept him, along with his circle of students, completely out of Russia during the revolution of 1917, and washed him onto Europe's shore. By the time he came to the notice of the West, this linguist, philosopher, traveller, dance instructor, musician, and mystic had evolved a system for the study and improvement of men, and had become one of the world's chief channels for esoteric doctrine. His name was George Gurdjieff.

One of the doctrines Gurdjieff incorporated into his teaching came from the wealth of mystical writings ascribed to the ancient Egyptian, Hermes Trismegistus. This is the same Hermes, of course, that figured so prominently in the thoughts of medieval alchemists sweating over the peculiar devices that were the ritual tools of their arcane art. This parallel isn't so strange when you compare the authentic teachings of alchemy, and their stress on inner transformation, with the ideas that Gurdjieff taught; they seem to have had many of the same goals in mind.

This particular doctrine describes the world as harmonious, objective, and unified. In this world everything is related to everything else by virtue of laws that apply equally to all scales of existence. The doctrine was expressed in a formula:

As above, so below.

Gurdjieff used this formula for the same reasons the alchemists did, perhaps even from the same point of view. He taught that every iota of reality was ruled by identical laws, and that a knowledge of how these laws affect a process on one level could also be used to understand similar processes on other levels. He called the laws that contained such universal power objective laws, and a good deal of his teaching rested on explaining and eventually understanding them.

When it came to the study of man, Gurdjieff's philosophy showed these laws in action. He taught that as long as a man remains ignorant of these laws, he will never find a way to manipulate them to his own advantage. Although Gurdjieff left almost no detailed knowledge of types behind him, he knew and studied the idea himself. Man's subjugation to the rigid, mechanical, and unyielding laws that he did describe is deeply embedded throughout the body of his thought.

Peter Ouspensky was one of Gurdjieff's chief pupils, and a member of the group that had followed him out of Russia. Later he recounted, in *In Search of the Miraculous,* his time with Gurdjieff. In this book Ouspensky drew the broad outline of the methods he had been shown by which men could learn to observe these laws themselves, and by which they could change.

Both Gurdjieff and Ouspensky saw the study of human psychology as an individual exploration into human evolution; the aim of their teaching was the creation of "higher" men. Like the alchemists, they reached far back into the history of practical mysticism for their materials, and there found what they required: concepts that would breathe life into their idea of human perfectability. They constructed models of man based on these ancient teachings, and used these models to put the tools of self-study, self-change, and self-realization into the hands of their students.

Although there are many detailed maps of human

psychology in the system Gurdjieff and Ouspensky taught, body types didn't receive much attention. It was one of Ouspensky's students, Rodney Collin-Smith, who finally gathered all the loose strands. Collin, an Englishman who moved to Mexico after Ouspensky's death in 1947, connected the old knowledge to new, and in his *Theory of Celestial Influence* laid the groundwork for the scheme of types.

One of the chief contributions Collin made in his description of types was to assemble a mass of apparently unrelated knowledge in one place. He rediscovered the work of Dr. Berman, and connected the insights of modern endocrinology to the lore of archaic priests and shamans. He hadn't set out to explain body types; he was determined to explain everything, and to unearth all the connections he could between modern science and the philosophy he'd inherited from Ouspensky.

In *The Theory of Celestial Influence* Collin set out the analogy that lies behind the theory of body types. In its present form, this analogy compares four different levels: the action and the interaction of the glands; the characteristics of the planets; the traits and ties of the archetypal gods, and the work and relationships of men. The shape of this analogy was formed by the parallels Collin found among its parts. Its force was supplied by the similarities in its disparate worlds of planets, gods, men, and glands.

But by adding the endocrine glands to the mix, Collin set his idea of types apart from earlier versions, and revitalized an ancient study. In many ways the connection between glands and behavior remains tantalizing, but out of reach. It promises new ways to comprehend men, but it's still clouded and inscrutable. Studying the glands helps us to understand types, however; it parallels the other worlds of the theory, and like them contains a variety of individuals organized into a complete, cohesive, and universal system that can be applied to anyone.

Everyone has all the endocrine glands, and the glands always contribute the same functions to the work of the body. The planets, moons, and other members of the solar system hang in their fixed relations in space. Society continues to make use of the work of different kinds of people. And each of us has within us all the primal urges that the old gods represented. Each member of each system—gland, planet, god, or man— always supplies the same kind of work within its community.

For an example, look at Mars, which is related to the adrenal glands. Humans can't live without their adrenals; they have too many unique and urgent jobs to do. The rush of adrenaline is a natural, necessary, human function. The war god Mars guards the borders, repels intruders, destroys the weak— that is, he stands for the guarding, repelling, destroying that are natural and necessary in every society. That planet that bears his name is the "red" planet, the "angry" planet. And it's the pugnacious Martial body type that contributes the warriors, the pioneers, and the fighters to humanity.

This theory reduces the types to seven different kinds; a number so small it threatens to squash any chance we had to be unique. But each of us is a different combination of the same, familiar features; our precise tuning and peculiar rhythms are what distinguish us as individuals. Blending the few basic types still creates the incredible diversity we see in people wherever we look. And while it might seem that studying types would crush one's sense of oneself, Rodney Collin, Peter Ouspensky, George Gurdjieff, and their ancestors, were actually working to promote a less mechanical, more spiritual, individuality.

Collin tried to indicate, in a general way, how to observe body types. This was very important, because the system that these three taught was based on direct experience and personal observation. In this system, known as the *Fourth Way*, if you can't verify the ideas yourself, they're useless. Body types, to be taken seriously, ought to be easy to see.

I've found that they are easy to see, that anyone can learn to grasp types if they search a little. Like all searches, this one begins best with the right tools, with a general idea of the types, and with some pointers left for us along the way by the people who have gone before.

*   *   *

One of the basic tools we use when studying body types is a diagram that George Gurdjieff introduced as

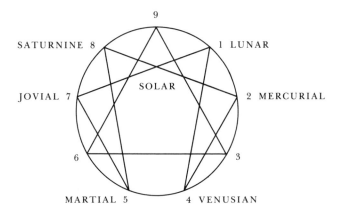

part of his philosophy. It consists of three separate figures merged into one, and is known as the *enneagram* because it has nine principle points. (The prefix ennea-stands for the number nine.)

The outside figure is a circle around which are nine equally spaced points. Each point is numbered. The topmost point is nine, the one to its right one, the next two, and so on clockwise around the circle. The second figure is the equal-sided triangle created by linking the points nine, six, and three. The third figure connects the remaining six points in the order; one, four, two, eight, five, seven. This yields a rising, crossing shape of six lines, independent of both outer circle and inner triangle. While Gurdjieff used this enneagram to illustrate many of his ideas about man, and much of his cosmology, we principally use the inner, six-pointed figure of the enneagram when studying body types.

Each type occupies one of these points except Solar,

which has no precise location. Lunar starts the progression at point one, and proceeding in the same order we used to generate this figure, we come to Venus at four, Mercury at two, Saturn at eight, Mars at five, and Jupiter at seven, from which point the figure completes itself by returning to one.

Within this scheme, pure types simply don't exist. Every one of us is situated at some point on this line of progression, and the unique blend of our type contains the influences of every type.

It's when we consider the types as archetypes, symbols of our primitive passions, that we have to look at them separately. Then they epitomize those passions, and the desires and perceptions potential in each of us. Isolated, the types become the separate but equal members of a pantheon, a set of glands, a planetary system, or a society of men. But the people we meet are amalgams in whom one type has been alloyed with a neighbor, and who show traces of them all.

This flow around the enneagram occupies one of the chief places in the idea of body types. Its direction determines the order of the types, and its structure implies many of their characteristics. The order is always the same, and we speak about types as developments within this order: Lunar, Lunar-Venusian, Venusian, Venusian-Mercury, and so on.

Let me show you what I mean by using myself as the example closest to hand. Since my body type is ruled by Jupiter and the Moon, I am a *Jovial-Lunar* type. Not a Lunar-Jovial. I can find occasional traits of Venus, or

Saturn, or the others, in my attitudes and behavior, but mostly what I see in myself arises about equally from Jovial and Lunar.

The structure that's described by the rhythmic, repetitive flow of the enneagram displays two of the basic traits of body types. These traits play an overriding part in determining the outline of our body and our general appearance. They regulate our thinking, skew our relationships, and color our most fundamental attitudes.

First, each type is either positive or negative, in the way that an electrical charge is positive or negative. This charge alternates through the flow of types, and starts at Lunar, a negative type. Venusian is positive, Mercury negative, Saturn positive, Mars negative, and Jovial positive. Solar, which doesn't participate in the circulation of types, is positive as well. Whether positive or negative, this trait slants our view of life and prejudices many parts of our behavior.

Simply put, positive types are more optimistic. They disregard the difficult and unpleasant sides of life, and seem to possess a generally constructive mentality. Negative types are more skeptical, restless, and dissatisfied. They take a dimmer, more careful view of life, and frequently can't avoid noticing its faults, its flaws, and its frequent failures.

The second basic characteristic of the types is how active or passive they are. Here the enneagram is divided differently; the active types are Mercury, Saturn and Mars, the passive ones are Jovial, Lunar, and Venusian. But these attributes don't alternate like the positive and negative ones did—activity and passivity, which also represent the masculine and feminine principles, wax and wane as they progress through the types, and subtly color each type's vitality and tone.

In this progression we find the energy and orientation of types at its most passive in Lunar. It continues to be passive through Venusian, enters the active sphere at Mercury, peaks in Saturn, and declines through Mars. Finally, it passes back across the threshold of passivity at Jovial, and the cycle is complete. Solar, outside this circulation, is an active type. Because the active, masculine force isn't static, but evolves through distinct stages under a variety of influences before it turns passive, each type represents a specific quality or mixture of these influences.

Mercury, for instance, still has traces of the feminine, while Jupiter has traces of the masculine. Venusians, whose minds and bodies are by far the quietest of all the types, also seem to be sunk deepest in passivity. But it's actually Lunar, with the passive energy of Jovial behind, and the passive energy of Venusian in front, that is the purest expression of the passive, feminine principle.

Again, although Mars accumulates the active energy, and is the most violently active type, and although Mercury carries activity that's young and rising from Venus, it is Saturn, despite its slow and introspective bearing, that occupies the primary active role, and that overflows

28

with the tide of masculinity as it flows between Mercury and Mars.

A simple way to understand the active and passive qualities of people is to look at the ways they use their time. A quiet Sunday afternoon finds one person cleaning his house or tinkering with his car. Someone else is satisfied to curl up with a good book and not go out all day. Those who must have something to do are usually active types.

The combination of active, passive, positive and negative traits yields four combinations for the seven types. Lunar is the only body type that's both passive and negative, while Saturn is its opposite, active and positive. Venusian and Jovial are passive, positive types, and are balanced by Mercury and Mars, both active and negative.

Active and positive people, Saturns and Solars, are full of plans, building houses, founding organizations, working on their careers, or recruiting friends to help with their many projects. Martials and Mercuries, active types who are also negative, are restless and don't need a reason to move; they're compelled. But wherever they go, trouble follows. They can't watch a movie without noticing the jumpy editing, they can't eat at a new restaurant without criticizing the service. They're glad to point out these defects to anyone who'll listen, and may pick a fight with you if you don't agree.

Venusians and Jovials, who are both passive and positive, are playful and popular. They're warm and generous, even benevolent. They're always there to help friends or strangers in a fix, whether it's a bowl of chicken soup that's needed, or ready cash. They can be sensuous and fun, but are often disorganized and lazy. Lunars, the only passive and negative type, are loners. They're unhappy with the way things are, but only contribute complaints. They think the weather's awful, their job's a bore, and life hardly worth living. As if being passive isn't enough, they lack either the desire to change anything, or the energy, or both.

The flow of the enneagram, however, also contains the remedy each of the types needs to overcome its particular imbalance. By looking toward the type ahead, and at the strengths inherent in that type, each will find exactly what it needs to offset its own weaknesses. For example, the Lunar who can't help keeping cool and distant, even in the storms of his own passion, will find in the warmth and openness of Venus an antidote, should he be able to acquire it, for his anguish.

We can also plot on the enneagram a picture of the forces that draw one type to another, or that repel them in disgust. Here, it's not surprising, opposites attract, and blends of opposites create blends of attraction.

Lying on opposing sides of the enneagram, the pairs of types that are drawn to each other have qualities that, when combined, strike an uneasy but fascinating attraction. Saturn, which is positive, active, and paternal, attracts and is attracted by negative, passive, and childish Lunar. Jovial's positive, passive flamboyance is the perfect complement to Mercury's negative, active wit. Mars finds in the receptive Venus a welcome for all his active, negative energy. Solar, a type that mixes with the other six, depends on that mixture to establish its attractions; they mostly correspond to those that already exist between the other types.

These three different bonds created by the three pairs of types are examples of universal kinds of relationships. The Lunar-Saturn bond stands for the push and pull of our connection to our family; it's undemonstrative but strong. The combination of Mercury and Jovial symbolizes our more social associations, like the waxing and waning of our circle of friends; here the emphasis is on variety, spontaneity, and wit. The tie that binds Mars to Venus vibrates with the intensity between lovers; it's where our most disturbing emotions are found.

Maybe each of us also has a type with which we just don't mix: the chemistry's all wrong. We repel each other with a natural force, and like the positive poles of two magnets we never get close enough to touch. Although we're aware enough of the other to exclude them, it's a hazy awareness, and undemanding. For us, these people just don't exist.

Mercury and Mars, however, the two active, negative types, repel each other more than any combination on the enneagram. Their instinctive repulsion is unreasoned, immediate, and violent. It is the opposition of forces that are too similar to mistake each other, and too different to endure each other. Their goals often look the same to everyone else, but because they're approaching these goals from contrary directions, they risk the explosive impact of a head-on collision.

Each of these attractions and repulsions is a dynamic connection, fueled by the tension of opposites. Each contains not only the material to create powerful desires, but the seeds of equally powerful distaste. At the same time, these combinations can illustrate our inner world as well, and describe the factions at war within us; then they tell us something about the nature of our own inner struggles.

⁂　⁂　⁂

If we could spot the type of the friend sitting on our couch, our boss at the office, our lover, father, or son, what exactly would we be seeing? Can we distinguish between characteristics that tell us their type and qualities that only individuals can possess? I think we can, but only if we remember that no matter how obvious a type seems to be, and no matter how abrupt our recognition of that type has been, there are no *typical* people.

Like any other method we might use to classify people, body types can be misunderstood, misrepresented, or misused. Then the ideas produce fraud, bias, or bigotry. These distortions aren't built into the idea of body types, but they happen anyway, because we confuse the types we see with the people in whom we're seeing them.

It's essential that we train ourselves to make this distinction. Without it we won't be able to learn about body

types, or use our knowledge to deepen our understanding of people. The honesty of a friend, for instance,
regularly and truly proved, is his alone, regardless of
his type. Maybe he's a Martial, a type noted for frank
comments and blunt evaluations. The hand of Mars will
guide the form his honesty takes, and make it strike a
frank and brutal note. Mars can't make him honest if
he isn't, any more than Mercury can make someone dis-
honest, if he's committed to truth.

You can see this distinction in the action of a
moment. If conditions demand this virtue from our
friend, it won't be Mars, but something deeper, more
personal, that will inspire him to be true to his conviction, to disregard his own chances, and tell you what he
thinks.

If we notice nobility, deceit, intelligence, flexibility
of mind, prejudice, courage, ambition, or grace in the
people we're observing, (or in ourselves, for that matter), we're seeing the signs of individuality—notes
struck deep inside the framework that's provided by a
body type.

I make a point of this distinction because in describing the types in the chapters ahead I have had to treat
them whole. These aren't portraits of specific people.
They're meant to suggest the themes that run through
the types, the atmosphere that surrounds them, and the
motives that drive them. The descriptions show the
kinds of desires that we owe to our body types, and the
means with which we pursue those desires. Although

they're abstractions, they're useful ones, and I invite you to use them to observe whomever you like.

*   *   *

People who study body types get a new angle on themselves almost immediately. They're jarred, and begin to see their own behavior in quite a different light. A person who starts to notice many signs of Jupiter in himself, for instance, will also start to wonder why he's so proud of his generosity. Or he may look at the friends he effortlessly collects in a new way, and realize that these friends may not know very much about him. He may begin to wonder, in fact, which of the qualities he's been so proud of are really his own.

While this Jovial has certainly had the edge taken off his pride, he's gained something as well. He no longer criticizes himself for rarely finishing projects, or for reading ten books at once; he knows that Jovials have a periodic nature. He finds an explanation for his wanton use of money. Although he's given up his pride in his typical, automatic acts, he's also dropped the burden of his equally automatic guilt.

The more a person's study of body types broadens, the more it contributes to his understanding. He can begin to clarify for himself the loves he's had, and the ones that he hasn't, by applying what he knows about the attractions between types. Misunderstandings don't surprise him when he's been studying the subjective, idiosyncratic views of each type. He can even find the traits

34

that might balance him, if he has an impulse toward self-improvement.

The ideas that lie within the study of body types have no trouble keeping pace with the variety of human activity. These ideas continue to fascinate the imagination, as they're fed by a constant stream of new observations. Whether scrutinizing the policies of an incumbent President, or questioning the piety of a Renaissance Pope, knowing about types supercharges our comprehension, clarifies our thoughts, and opens the door to an entirely new way of looking at people.

Someone who continues with this study may begin to glimpse the enneagram of types everywhere, like a complex and subtle symbolism underlying the whole fabric of society. Cataloging all the possibilities of this symbolism would certainly fill several books; maybe a few examples will reveal the scope of its influence.

Look at the way the ideal of beauty has oscillated over the centuries. Why is it so difficult today to admire the robust and playful women in the paintings of Rubens? Perhaps the influence of each type, in turn, cycles through a period of dominance in society; if so, it may have swung away from these fleshy creatures. Today it is Saturn that rules our esthetics. We may be living through one of the few ages of human history in which Saturnine women have been considered the epitome of feminine beauty, an age in which the dreams of millions of men have been populated by women who are aggressive, angular, and vaguely masculine.

Or we could try to plot various roles in society on

the plan of body types. Here the symbols of the types express the different kinds of work that men do, and which help to construct a varied, complete society. Lunar contributes persistent work and eccentricity; Venus is the type of growth, breeding and care; Mercury acts as a conduit for the intellect, and holds the edge of crime; Saturn stabilizes the whole and governs it; Mars wages war, guards the realm, and pioneers new territories; Jupiter teaches, amuses, heals, and binds society together; Solar adds charisma and sparkle to the lot.

Whole nations and races of people can be diagnosed according to this grammar of types. The long and insular history of the Chinese suggests they are a lunar race; secretive, willful, and inscrutable. Or the history of the British, who have contributed to our ideas of fairness and justice while dominating whole continents: it's a picture of the type that stretches from Saturn to Mars. Or the inventive, quick and animated manner of the Japanese may put us in mind of dexterous Mercury.

On and on we could go, and the theory of body types would continue to spring at us from all directions. We can never use it up. Wandering over its vast and detailed landscape we're humbled, surprised, and enlightened by turns, but we're never bored. Each observation, each understanding underscores the reality of types, and propels us to more exact observations, deeper understandings.

Finally, we begin to grasp how potent and pervasive a tool we've inherited. It's a tool that achieves its greatest effect when it deepens our insight into ourselves, when it shows us quite new boundaries between the false and the real within us. That is when the outlines of the types emerge from the mists of wordy description, and begin to take on the familiar features of the world we have always lived within, but which we are only just beginning to see.

LUNAR

LUNAR FEELINGS, LIKE STILL WATERS, run deep. A Lunar may be alive with inner excitement, but to others show only a faint blush. Those who have tried to open the secrets of a Lunar come away shaking their heads in frustration, or in dismay. It seems that the more you want a Lunar to speak, the stronger his resistance becomes, and it can become perverse. Like the Cheshire cat in *Alice in Wonderland*, a Lunar can disappear just when you think he's about to tell you everything, and leave you with only a trace of his smile lingering in your mind.

Anyone who's had dealings with Lunars can tell you how they react to new ideas: they resist. The accepted strategy for dealing with Lunars is this: prepare yourself for "no" as the first response to any request. And the second. The third time around you may find out how they actually feel about what you've asked; you've helped them work the "no" out of their systems.

A Lunar's power isn't very hard to see: try telling him to do something he doesn't want to do. When he refuses, as he probably will, you'll see a negative form of power. It's not the power to make other people do what he wants, it's the power of an obstacle that can't be moved. Like all power, it revolves around control.

Lunars' power is dedicated to not being controlled just the way that more active forms of power are dedicated to controlling; being in command is what concerns them both. When these two forms of power meet, it's an irresistible force meeting an immovable object. And somehow, they exist for each other. Lunars need someone to refuse, to disobey, to ignore; they rely on more active types to rouse both their resistance, and the heady feeling of independence that comes with it.

This power also has a positive side to it. When a Lunar has an aim he isn't easily distracted. He focuses on what he wants to do, and fortifies himself against anything outside this narrow range. This persistence is an attractive trait of Lunar, and it's probably the best weapon Lunars have in their struggle to overcome a passivity so strong that it can make them numb.

Lunars are negative in an offhand, involuntary way. To them, events are awful, people difficult, the job a bore, and the outlook dim. So what can you expect? Without question, things will turn out poorly; in the meanwhile you can only sigh and get on with it—that's their position.

You can't underestimate this ability of Lunar to interpret life darkly. A bump to his habitual pessimism will crack this cloud cover for a moment, allowing a sunny ray of optimism to shine through. More often, he will insist on his own moody insight. He's convinced that his efforts will end in doom, failure or humiliation—a certainty that can keep him from committing himself. He feels that he's a person who is bound to fail, and this feeling darkens his whole view of the world. Even so, there are some Lunars in whom ambition, or an over-riding hope, splits their constant pessimism, and thrusts them into action.

Depressed people isolate themselves, building psychological walls within which their dissatisfaction can ferment. Maybe it's this kind of barrier that estranges Lunars from the rest of us. They don't mix easily in society, and consider themselves outcasts, misunderstood and harried by more outgoing types. Their aloofness constricts them. Behind it lies fear and the frustration of social paralysis. To us, the same aloofness supplies Lunars with an air of mystery; they seem inscrutable, opaque.

This is a type that exaggerates its isolation in many ways. Lunars wear dark clothes that they hope will make them invisible, or at least, anonymous. Their humor is childish, too simple, and somehow unfunny to anyone else. You'll see them snickering to themselves in the corners of rooms, where they can see anyone who's coming, and where, if they're lucky, they may not be noticed.

In the middle of a conversation they'll smirk at something you've said, and if pressed to tell you why, their explanation of what tickled them still escapes you—there's just nothing funny in it. Lunars giggle at absurdities. They are the people you hear in dark movie houses laughing at all the poignant, or at all the wrong, places.

It's not hard to see why Lunars meet so much resistance when they try to overcome this social deformity. Their type lacks either an active part, or a positive one. Lunar is the only negative, passive body type; an existence that can't be easy. They're so uncomfortable with social initiatives that their efforts turn them into supplicants, or sycophants, or lend them an abrupt, dismissive tone. They're too scared to be confident, and too wrapped in themselves to see the effect they're having. Without some jolt from necessity, or without a favorable circumstance, they slide back into inertia, go back behind the walls.

Lunars hide themselves, their ideas, and their activities more than anyone else. They're not compelled, like others, to advertise themselves, and don't need your approval for motivation. Besides being naturally shy, they doubt you're interested in them anyway. A Lunar will come to suspect your motives if you show any interest in his life or his thoughts, and in many cases he's right to be suspicious. A slow, hidden, childish and unsocial person does seem to most people a bland dish, and Lunars are often pursued for more impersonal, or more functional reasons—their expertise in some craft, or the doggedness they'll bring to your project if you can convince them to help.

It's not just their bland personalities that make Lunars look colorless to others. They have a black-and-white view of the world—grey areas, confusion, and discrimination are tuned out of their picture. If it isn't right, it must be wrong. What isn't good has no ambiguity—it's simply bad. Moods carry them along on a swell of feeling from one extreme to another, from childish expectation to depression, from persistent action to despair. You can't shake a Lunar out of his moods, and he can't either.

If Lunars are difficult to deal with, and they are, it's because they've become rooted in these extremes, and their nature tells them not to budge. They get cantankerous and willful. Catch them in a state like this and all your persuasion will only make them more rigid and unyielding. They won't bow to conventions of behavior or commonly-held assumptions.

Lunars' odd habits and manners place them outside what we think of as normal. They look peculiar to us, but not to themselves; they have their own curious logic to support them. All the types throw off an occasional eccentric, but Lunar is the only eccentric body type. His eccentricity distinguishes the Lunar to himself, and fuels his sense of isolation.

We admire Lunars for their persistance, a never-quit approach to something they've once started. With their company, their country, or their ideas, this persistance manifests as loyalty, and makes them tough and dependable. All the narrowness of their thinking then becomes constructive and makes them firm supporters, tireless workers for their cause. On the pledge of their devotion you need never doubt—they'll be with you to the end.

The Lunar is not a vibrant type, and they won't grab your eye in passing. The women have a doe-like look, and really don't want to attract attention. The men seem vulnerable, with a limpid sensitivity that magnifies their femininity. When not dressed in black, they wear odd colors, in odd combinations. They like small, detailed prints, lace, and ruffles. They give you the impression of being outside fashion, even if only by half-a-step. They can put together a chic look sometimes, but the effect is either too timid or too forceful, and you don't think they'll ever get it quite right.

Lunar beauty isn't much appreciated these days, even though the sculptures in which an attempt has been made to carve a perfect female form, especially the Aphrodites of Greece, owe the type a great deal. We see in them the soft curves, delicate proportions, and dewy skin of the ideal Lunar woman. No other type can approach the ideal Lunar's utterly perfect and feminine form. But in life, many Lunars inhabit odd and childish bodies. They seem unfinished, as if they were made of a lumpy dough, or they have a cramped, owlish face, and look old beyond their age.

It's easy to like Lunars; you want to protect them. Those tall, judicial types we frequently see them with are Saturns searching for someone to protect, someone to save. Saturns are the opposite of Lunars; they're active where Lunars are passive, masculine where Lunars are feminine, public where Lunars are private. Both Lunars and Saturns are lured to exactly what they themselves don't possess, and see in each other the material for their own completion. Like father and child, Saturn and Lunar create a stable atmosphere that puts us in mind of long-lived family connections. It's not an atmosphere of passion and abandon.

Of course, this is a connection that easily unites Saturnine men with Lunar women. For a Saturn woman, on the other hand, Lunar men may seem baffling. These women are frightened by a Lunar's coolness, and frustrated by his inactivity. A Lunar's sweetness and quiet intimacy pull on deep needs of Saturn, but in the world of action Lunars often seem ineffectual and slow.

The connection between these types strains with an extreme reversal of the roles we've been taught, and it may appear grotesque. The Saturn women can't make themselves happier by sacrificing their initiative and activity, and Lunar men maim themselves by dressing up in an ill-fitting ambition. It's not a surprise that few of these relationships bloom. Their failure serves to reinforce the Lunar's pessimism; it suits his melancholy nature, and it feeds his brooding, poetic turn of mind.

The coolness that so infuriates us in Lunars, their ability to ignore us completely, to remain aloof, to hide their feelings, also has another side. You'll see it in times of stress or danger when others are tossed here and there by their own reactions to crises, and when Lunars remain composed, unmoved. Their natural restraint may keep them away from chatty parties, but it also puts them at a distance from passions that overpower others.

Their uncanny detachment opens to Lunars feats of selflessness and courage, like calmly walking into a burning room to carry out a trapped child. Their responses in emergencies are often calmly reasoned and pragmatic, and carried out with aplomb.

This certainty surfaces in their conversation as well. A Lunar has already reduced his perceptions to extremes, a reduction that gives everything he says the heavy thud of fact, no matter how inane or eccentric his opinion may be. Whether right or wrong, he sounds right, and convinces people by his tone of infallibility.

The dark ages give off a finicky Lunar air. When I think of the rigid ties of feudal serf to feudal lord, and the isolation of communities cut off from one another, I'm reminded of Lunar. It was an age that glorified God, but was overwhelmed by its own pessimism. Activity seems to have been very circumscribed, and life itself perpetually overcast. Even the darkness of the age reminds me of the subterranean air of Lunars, permanently turned away from both society's light and the companionship of others. It even reminds me of the dark, invisible clothing they wear. In the medieval monasteries we get a glimpse of Lunar at work.

Imagine a monk bent over his manuscript in the scriptorium of some abbey and appreciate his humble dedication to the copying of old texts. This detailed, painstaking work, devoid of fame or recognition, seems to me one height of Lunar's anonymous toil, and gives me a feeling for the age.

Study some of the medieval ivories, carved in religious devotion, or the intricate boxwood balls made by these monks, and you'll get this feeling too. Boxwood, dense and hard, can be worked to an extremely fine level of details. In one of these carvings, about the size of a baseball, you might see a vast panorama; the countryside in the foreground gives way to a city scene in the background, where merchants, soldiers, and holy processions compete for space. In the fields the peasants toil, and in the city individual buildings are microscopically described. No matter how hard you look, you can't find those spots where the particular breaks down and gives way to the texture of the wood itself.

There's a touch of lunacy here. A low but insistent whisper of madness and confusion echoes in your mind when you try to figure out the motives, let alone the methods, of the artists who created such puzzles. This uncanny and self-sacrificing devotion strikes me as an emblem of Lunar.

In more modern times, Lunars use the same abilities and dedication that the monks used, but in research, or in libraries where they coolly pore over dusty tomes crammed with esoteric data. They're anonymous and diligent back-office workers, precise and confident with books and numbers. They squint in the light of publicity or acclaim, and can't wait to return to the solitude of their studies. Lost in the smallest parts of their subject, Lunars rely on others to work out the implications of what they've found. Their infatuation is with breaking things down, discerning smaller and smaller quantities to be named, analyzed and related, not in building up a view of the whole.

The paintings of the seventeenth-century Dutch

painter Jan Vermeer often remind me of Lunar, and especially those of lonely or isolated women, serene in some corner of their home. These women have a beautiful softness, or a childish reserve that's Lunar. From up close the studied detail of rugs draped over tables, or the clarity of maps tacked to the walls, is dazzling. The whole scene is distant, separated from us forever by an invisible detachment. The people in these paintings don't invite us to share the moment that's been captured here, but remain self-absorbed, untouchable.

The landscapes of Jean-Baptiste Camille Corot give me another insight into Lunar. These pastoral scenes are delicately colored, hazy and poignant. We want to watch the world from here, protected by the deep shade of an overhanging tree, and have no desire to venture out into the light.

Lunars, like nocturnal animals, populate late-night cities, and can be observed as they slink quietly down deserted streets, or stare out from behind the counter of some all-night coffee shop. They embody a more primitive life, one in which it was only safe in the cave, and darkness hid the dangers of the day.

A Lunar's home can give you a subterranean chill. Pull aside the drapes of his dimly lit room, and you may be in for a surprise. You're just as apt to find a fantastic view as you are an airshaft; he just doesn't care about what's outside. He would rather arise late in the day, to a cool, darkened den.

Lunars put me in mind of owls or ferrets or, occasionally, rabbits; mostly creatures that live close to the ground. Their ability to survive among larger, more powerful predators stirs my admiration for their persistence and self-reliance. Lunars are tough, it's true, and shot through with stubbornness. But besides their timidity, they have an innocence that makes them endearing, and prompts a tenderness in the rest of us that is truly their own.

VENUSIAN

LIKE LUNAR, VENUSIAN IS PASSIVE and feminine. However, Venusian is positive and receptive where Lunar is negative and unreceptive, and it is this combination that dominates Venusians and gives them their tone.

Venusians seem to be able to accept almost anyone, no matter how lame, ill, or ugly the victims might be. Any living thing can wrench hold of their attention, and the more that help is needed, the more strongly will a Venusian respond. The complete lack of judgment that makes this possible is one of the Venusian's most attractive traits.

This unjudging acceptance places Venusians close to the world of nature, where the beautiful coexists with the barbaric. The variety we see in natural things isn't moral, or good; it's simply diverse, containing numberless forms, colors, sizes, and materials within its teeming fabric.

Nature's complexity can produce, for instance, the poise and beauty of California's coastline. But nature also spawns the restless forces that arise and lay waste to the rolling hills; the waves that batter the shore, the rains that rip away the soil, and the heaving earth that tears itself apart. Our bodies have also been made from nature's materials. But from the same materials nature has made the bacteria that swarm through this frame when it's alive, and that reclaim it for nature when it dies.

Venus displays the same rude equality as the natural world does. Venusians don't choose one person over another; they accommodate everyone. They are generous, open and undiscriminating, sometimes to an unfortunate degree.

Generosity demands that we surrender a bit of ourselves for someone else's good. But how much can we give before we start to cut into what we are, the sources of our identity? Most of us have a clear idea of this boundary, and get wary when we're near it. We resist what we think will blur the outlines of our personality, and pull back.

Venusians aren't so worried. Discrimination seems like cruelty to them, and the contour of their character blurs as they surrender home, clothes, time, and attention to anyone who asks. They will give up their own interests in favor of yours. They'll let the subject you introduce in conversation force out their own, and won't even notice. They think less of their opinions than anyone else does, and demand little from their friendships. Their dreams of glory most often put them next

50

to someone famous; not in the spotlight, but in its shadow.

Their own goodness victimizes them. A Venusian gives up his own desires, his own thoughts, and his own individuality at the same time. He shies away from asserting himself, and doesn't want to make decisions. His slide into passivity robs him of the clearly defined character that other types get from exercising their personalities. Acceptance saps his force and dilutes his very considerable warmth. At their lowest, Venusians become little more than living matter. Whatever they say or do lacks force, and doesn't stick. You might say that they *cease to exist.*

You won't find a Venusian alone much—he wilts in isolation. Sitting apart, his already smooth, featureless face tends to go slack. He's flaccid when there's no one to charge him with vitality. He prefers a mob crowding around, and the warmth of all those bodies. In seclusion he can't find anything to do with himself, and gets panicked by having to make the most ordinary decisions; should he do the laundry first, or should he go shopping?

This type has an incessant need for contact; not affection but proximity. Like a pet you've grown accustomed to, you're likely to find them snuggled next to you, their shoulder on yours, hips touching. They'll coerce you into all the hugs and kisses, pats and cuddles you can stand, and more, to get some energy they don't generate themselves. They're always attaching themselves to one host or another, like creeping vines, or bright-faced bougainvillaea, climbing up you to get the sunshine they need. Or maybe they're trying to speed up their lagging metabolism. They are, of all the types, the slowest.

Any Venusian may suddenly ask you for a massage, or offer to give you one. Saturns have this habit too, but for them its simply another way they might be able to improve you. Venusians want to make you feel better, and they want to get all that fleshy contact that goes with the job.

One of the keys to their universal popularity is that you don't have to be interested in what they did today; they're happy if you're just in the room with them. Where else will you find someone who's glad to feed you, happy to touch you, eager for the details of your triumphs and stumbles? Someone who won't bore you with his own stories, or interrupt you to disagree with your opinion? Only on Venus. Why shouldn't Venusians be popular?

Venusians get us to confide in them, and tell them all our deepest secrets. It's surprising how easy and confident a Venusian can make us feel. We gladly confess the most humiliating incidents of our lives when faced with their benign acceptance. Since they don't compete with us, don't begrudge our wider fields of interest, it scarcely matters that they don't need to understand us either. No matter how stupid or inept we're feeling, no matter how frequent our social gaffes, it only takes a Venusian nearby to dissolve our self-judgement with warmth and acceptance.

52

Venusians are detached in their generosity, almost indifferent. They're concerned with so many people that individuals don't matter as much as we might think. Their hunger is for people on whom to lavish their care; they attract whichever "victims" will feed it. Oddly enough, it's this indifference that's partly responsible for the comfort they bring us; we know we're not being judged for our flaws, and we're able to accept ourselves. We feel cleansed, healed, self-confident again, and back on our feet.

The more you see Venusians the more clearly you see this lack of independence, and lack of focus, in them. They weigh heavily on the people to whom they attach themselves. By converting the ideas and concerns of a friend, teacher, or mate into their own, they attempt to shine by the light reflected there, a satellite glowing but cold. The energy they draw off their host is food for the life on the surface of their personality, and it's food that they can't do without.

You can count on getting a friendly reception from a Venusian no matter how long it's been since you last saw him. Walk in on an old friend like this and he'll only want to put you at your ease, make you as fat and happy as he is. He'll still be as loyal as an old dog, and as comfortable as your bedroom slippers.

It's important to a Venusian to feel comfortable. They want clothes that are loose and cozy, that feel good. They like touching and being touched. They run their hands over the furniture, caress the vegetables in the sink, and curl up with their pets, or children, for frequent naps. It takes something pricking their senses to make them feel alive. They can't cook without sticking their fingers in the food; if you weren't watching, they'd bathe in it. They get a look of bliss when they're up to their elbows in dough, or mashing potatoes through their fingers.

Sensuality propels Venusian eroticism, not passion, or lust. It's the warmth of the body that they love, its textures and smells. They are not trying to conquer you with sex, like some types, nor do they try to obliterate their own personality, like others. They use sex for its sensuality, its closeness; it's a natural joy they get, like a child's, and it doesn't put us off.

Painters have capitalized on this sensuality. Venusians lounge in a languorous mist of sated passions on cushions and divans in the art of many periods. They're frank and open, gazing at us with a proud look of unabashed sensuality. Their dewy femininity finds its way into paintings of famous erotics and lovers, whether gazing as expectantly as Danaë, or with the casual, dismissive glance of an odalisque. Titian, for example, fashions their bodies into satiny boudoir pillows. François Boucher makes them look as if they've been deboned, leaving only enough of a skeleton to keep the moist flesh suspended, trembling.

Venusians give off a humid air of sensuality and remind us of the steamy earthiness of the Mediterranean world whether they come from Venice or Vancouver. The thick, dark hair on many Venusians' bodies—both men and women—heightens this impression. The sensuality that makes them artistic and intuitive lovers is as natural a force as the tides, and as regular. They're free from many of the insecurities and fears that cloud others' enjoyment of life's physical side.

Venusians get a simple, animal pleasure from their senses. They surround sex with a luxurious mist of sensation. And yet they can get caught up in sensuality and become victimized by it, all too easily swept away in a rush of sensations. Their emotions then have little play exactly where they are most needed; they've been pushed into the background by earthier drives. The balance that the mind can bring, being more fragile, has already vanished.

Venusians wield the power of passivity. The strength that they have comes from constancy, and through it Venusians overcome stronger, but more cyclical forces. From classical ages Venus is shown as the conqueror of Mars, her lover and adversary, through this power. Mars may rage with passion, but he can't last forever. Artists show us the war god who, having fought the noble fight in Venus' arms, has reached the end of his energy. There he lies, pitifully, spent and at Venus' feet. The radiant goddess looks on—sometimes with a smirk.

By a similar method Venusians exert a considerable force on people and events, but it's a force that's difficult to gauge. Their steady pressure can smother you even though it appears benevolent. It's the same way a growing tree that provides you with shade and beauty can bring down your house by growing right through the walls. The strength in this process may surprise you when it rises to the surface from beneath a Venusian's slow and gentle personality—what's surprising is that it feels so inevitable.

We're used to seeing power in explosive, compelling acts, and are unprepared for the resolve that lies beneath a Venusian's passivity. You'd think a type as passive as Venus would be easily distracted by the powerful currents of life, thrown by more active people. But it isn't always true; Venusians just have a longer view, which gives them more time to get their way.

Slow, natural growth rules many of a Venusian's activities. Thriving plants crowd their homes and contribute to the relaxed, messy ambiance. Somehow it's not surprising to find a Venusian cooing to the cucumbers in his garden, or encouraging his coleus to take its medicine. He doesn't doubt his ability to communicate with either kids or trees by way of some instinctive language no one else is able to decipher.

In the city you'll find Venusians mooning over their flower boxes, and in the suburbs they're out planting bushes, or in the pay of a landscaper. Plants need the regular care that comes so easily to Venusians, and pull on their affections like members of the family.

Home and household exert a powerful pull on Venusians. They raise children as competently as they grow plants. They like the close connections built into family life, and the nurturing it requires. A family gives them something to belong to, and a whole crowd to look after. Their children don't lack for love, or for reassurance; they're more likely to be smothered by affection than driven by ambition. Venusians forgive their children everything, trying to heal with warmth what others might correct with discipline.

Venusians don't get restless often. They've already got a job, so why look for another? Their apartment isn't so great, but it's more comfortable than moving. They feel safe with familiar things, and don't need the excitement of an unknown city, a new career, or a dangerous adventure to make their blood run faster. They get high on people, on animals, on the shared reliance of a social mob. Their roots go deep into the loamy soil of their lives, and aren't easily or painlessly transplanted. They shrug off the thirst for exotic, strange, or uncomfortable experiences that animates more difficult types, and find satisfaction curled up in their favorite overstuffed chair, where everything's within easy reach.

Venusians pay a price for being so easily satisfied. Sometimes they give me the feeling that they were created quickly, without sharp corners or a detailed finish; they were never brought into focus. They present us with a pleasant but hazy profile; the people you can't remember from a party, or whose face never connects with a name. They are the kids that get forgotten when sides are being chosen, but don't let it get in the way of their loyalty.

In a group they'll smile and nod, and don't mind being interrupted. They're looking for someone to agree with, not for a fight. Venusians see the logic in everyone's arguments, but have little to offer of their own besides support. They'd like everyone to get along and have a good time. The principles for which some people will take a stand, risking a rancorous attention, just don't seem that important.

Naïveté comes along with all this goodness, and blinds Venusians to the squalor and infamy of life. Instead of trusting, they become gullible, and get teased by everyone. Naïveté makes them an easy mark for con men, and fiery preachers. They are charged with their desire to belong, and hold firm in their belief in everyone's goodness. Ignorant of the dark motives of manipulators, they allow their own interests to get squeezed out, and find that they've been used.

Venusians adopt the logic of a cause without worrying about its deeper ambiguities. They willingly become devotees, and in the unfortunate event that they're abused for it, still won't rebel against their manipulators. It's sad but common to see a Venusian determined to rehabilitate the salesman who's just swindled an outrageous sum of money out of him. He thinks this wretch is himself a victim who would come to his senses if he only received enough care; any defects the Venusian finds in a greedy or criminal personality he is sure can be cured by applying great dollops of sweetness and understanding.

Venusians lack the tautness of a well-defined character. There's no tension to give force to their personality, and little tone to their actions. They aren't compelled to have opinions, or convert you to their way of thinking. Browbeating them won't do any good—it only confuses their efforts to please you. They'll express an opinion if you like, but they're just as willing to abandon it if necessary for one more popular. The contradictions that force us to struggle to a unique understanding have little affect on Venusians, who really excel at staying relaxed and loose in all situations.

This general lack of tone strikes deep into their lives and makes their bodies soft, their habits slothful, and their minds inert. You'll find a Venusian laying on his couch, food scattered around, everything a bit mussed. He's at home with the entropy of his little universe, and doesn't see much reason to do anything about it; after all, it's natural. Mention to him the clothes he's got on, or point to the tracks his dinner left as it toppled down his dressing gown, and he's mildly surprised; he hadn't noticed.

This must be the only type that can leave the house wearing unmatched socks, or a dress inside out, and when it's mentioned be neither particularly astonished, nor too upset by the lapse. Venusians float through their day in something of a muddle, and no matter how much they spend on clothes always seem poorly put together. Within five minutes a Venusian can make a shirt fresh from the store look comfortable; give him ten minutes, and it will be positively rumpled.

Their sloth, passivity, and unfocussed geniality create profound difficulties for Venusians. They slide easily into a vacant space inside themselves that feels both comatose and secure. Pressure will drive them to this space, or stress, or fatigue. Watch them in front of the television, at the movies, or over dinner. If they think no one is looking, their eyes glaze over, their mouths fall slightly open, their muscles go limp.

In this state there are no opinions, no desires, no thoughts, and no responsibilities. Everything that's unique, unusual, interesting, all the idiosyncracies that might make them truly human, slip away. Personality has vanished, and taken individuality along with it even while you watch. Only the body remains behind. They're on hold, in neutral, something like the blank but active screen of a TV test pattern.

It's in this state that Venusians become victims. They defend themselves against violence, injustice and ill-will by surrendering their existence. Wrapping themselves in a void of not knowing, not caring, they hope it has made them invulnerable by making them invisible. They look for sanctuary from their faults and from the warts of the world by tuning in to some private void for a while. They want to rid themselves of whatever is objectionable by the same method.

It's a poor defense, and self-defeating; it leaves a Venusian nothing with which to fight, nothing with which to gather his strength. He descends naturally into oblivion—it's a habit. When he snaps back, he may not even know what's happened. You have to fill him in like an amnesiac who occasionally loses track of time.

Venusian loyalty strengthens the web of society. They support social groups of all kinds from companies to frat houses to local churches. Reliability strengthens them, and allows them to contribute their support and care. Venusians gravitate to the healing professions;

they become exemplary doctors, nurses, and caretakers. They get a charge from food, and cook creatively. They like to work in an office where they don't have to move around too much, but sometimes fall into rough and dangerous jobs when they try to fabricate an active personality, or imitate their opposite type, the Martial.

Although we can be put off by Venusians when they are hazy or indistinct, they endear themselves to us by their supple generosity, their healing warmth, and their genuine kindness. Venusians confront a formidable task when they try to change their nature and its habitual responses. But they dull the harshness of the world for the rest of us, and ease our progress through life.

MERCURIAL

AS WE LEAVE VENUS we proceed into the range of the active, or masculine, body types. Mercury, a negative type, is the first, followed by Saturn and Mars. Mercury combines these trends in quite a different way than does Mars, the other active, negative type. Both can be self-interested and manipulative, but in distinct and different ways. Mercury schemes, while Mars attacks; where Mercury is devious, Mars is likely to be blunt and brutal. Each of them influences other people with ease, but with opposing styles. You may be bullied by a Martial, but a Mercury will trick you with his sleight-of-hand and convincing voice. Speed and perceptiveness are what typify Mercury.

You won't have any trouble locating Mercuries; they want to be seen. Restless, quick and inquisitive, they love the spotlight. Everything about a Mercury, his curly hair, small frame, finely made hands and feet, and distinct features, is in constant movement. He has the agility of an athlete, and the animation of an actor, and all his roles are active. Indeed, a Mercury's approach to life may become like that of an actor to his script, as he struts and frets his imagined hour upon the stage.

Mercuries dress for effect, glitter for attention. They're always at center stage, each scene in their life crashes into the next, and drama is everywhere. Their eyes roam constantly, keeping track of all the reactions around them, like an insecure actor worried about losing his audience. Mercuries have the thespian's flourishes to match, and a deep voice that surprises you when it comes rolling out of such a small person. When they get turned on they're devious and cunning, constantly hatching plots, or confidentially hissing asides to let us in on their complicated schemes.

Lusting for fame, sick for glory, Mercuries have no difficulty standing out in a crowd. They announce their perfection without the hesitation that you or I might feel. But they watch for your response; do you admire their excellence as profoundly as they do themselves? They won't trust your affection if you don't approve of them, and they won't trust your judgment if you do. After all, they know it's all an act; why can't you see it? If you do see it, they're gone.

Every Mercury has a bit of the orator, the actor, the revolutionary in him. Like them, he's endlessly selling. And he's a terrific salesman, persuading us with his charm, his wit, and his sparkling eyes; it's not his sincerity we prize him for. A Mercury's wit flashes quick, and sometimes sharp. He can use his genius at mimicry to become a marvelous mime. Only his yen for approval, his constant need to be liked, tarnishes his otherwise admirable presentations.

Although Mercuries entertain us with their wit and cheer us with their sunniness, it's just as easy for them to suspect us of treason, or take a dark and apocalyptic view of their own future. Despite their outward radiance, their distrust and pessimism reveal the darker sides of a negative body type.

Lunars are negative also, but passively. For instance, they dig in their heels when pushed, but are compliant if left alone. Mercuries don't wait for someone to set them off. They have plans to actualize, and methods for getting what they want. While the lengths they're willing to go to for their ambitions differ as much as individuals and their private motives differ, Mercuries itch to rule the people and events that appear necessary to their mission.

For some Mercuries, the desire for control that underlies many of their aspirations can become their chief desire, guarded zealously by a habitual, vast, and consistent suspicion.

Perceptiveness joined to suspicion nudges Mercuries towards paranoia. They despise victims, and dread becoming one. They stay alert for the plots they know exist, and are constantly trying to ferret out the information that might save them.

They pick up tidbits of information the rest of us would find meaningless, or banal. Questions asked by a Mercury have the uncomfortable edge of an interrogation in which what you say, or the tone of your voice, or the way you hold your drink are no longer trivial, and may be used against you. A Mercury can make you wonder if you've said too much, or not enough, to justify yourself.

Since even a Mercury doesn't know all his own needs or all the motives that drive him, he may be right to be suspicious; maybe he's seen something we've simply missed. But he'll leave us uncertain, unable to refute his charges, and equally unable to believe them.

All this suspicion makes for a treacherous journey through life. Mercuries are convinced that some anonymous force has mined their road with pitfalls and is just waiting to spring a few clever traps. Their deepest fear is the fear of losing control. Nothing makes them more edgy than a situation in which they have no say, or one in which they have to obey the orders issued them. They see in these predicaments the certainty of being treated unfairly, or being rudely victimized. To protect themselves they demand their rights and responsibilities be pointed out to them.

Mercuries study rules, laws, and regulations, and work out loopholes no one has ever seen before. They can't stand the idea that someone found a better buy on a car, or made a more profitable marriage. Although they don't trust what you tell them, they'll still worry about what you haven't told them, and wonder why you're holding out.

They can't imagine that anyone else is concerned for their benefit, only for their downfall. One of the principles that guides a Mercury through life is the belief that everyone is acting from self-interest. This he never doubts, and will accuse his boss, a friend, or his mother of scheming against him. Nothing delights a Mercury more than having gotten a better deal than you did; when you're naïve about his motives his childish glee at getting the better of you seems adorable.

One way to get an example of this over-riding suspicion is by giving a Mercury a gift. You can almost see the wheels turning as he tries to figure out what you paid for it, and what you're going to ask for in return. He may be sure he deserves your generosity for being such a wonderful guy; he may even be thrilled by getting something free; but the anxiety you've caused makes him lose him poise. In his world, there are no simple actions, and he assumes that everyone's motives are obscure.

Assaulted by suspicion, Mercuries become circumspect and wary. They have difficulty trusting their friends or confiding in their mates. Their quick minds may well be several steps ahead of yours, but rampant uncertainties shake their confidence. They are never quite sure of the value of their own perceptions. So many things seem possible to a Mercury, he can't commit himself completely. Instead, racing here and there to hedge his bets, he tries to cover every eventuality.

Complexity doesn't daunt them, however, the way it might addle your mind or mine. Rather than resenting it, Mercuries make good use of complexity. It's their quick control over intricate arguments and their command of jargon that make conversation thrilling for a

Mercury, and safe. Whether the subject is politics or poetry, he charges ahead, convinced you'll never be able to keep up. He covers his tracks, flings clouds of obscurities to keep you from finding out his secrets. Complexity becomes a drug he uses to keep away the curious, who may wish him harm, and the simple, whom he disdains.

Of course, from one point of view their suspicions are on target: after all, there are a lot of other Mercuries out there, and no telling what schemes they're hatching right now.

It would be absurd to say that Mercuries are criminal, because crime belongs to individuals, not to categories of people. But it is also true that there is no other type in which crime finds so little resistance. Petty misdemeanors are habitual. They come home with pens from the office or tools from the shop, without realizing they've made off with someone else's property. Sidewalk stands present goods for the taking, if you're keen enough not to be caught. It's a morality that rewards their speed, their circumspection, and above all, their cleverness.

You could say that this is another example of the childish side of Mercury, where moral and ethical concerns don't carry the weight they do for more mature types. Maybe it's the elasticity of their morals that's on display. It's certainly a convenience—even a luxury— for a Mercury to have such flexible principles. He must have a great deal of faith in them, because no one else's principles seem to stretch quite as far as a Mercury's, nor quite as willingly.

I admire the assurance and optimism of Mercuries, perhaps because I neither organize nor advertise myself as rigorously as they. They always progress on schedule, no matter how often the schedule needs to be changed. If you attempt to pin them down, you'll get a chance to watch them wriggle and squirm their way off your hook. If they couldn't keep their options open, their plans fluid and their movement unhindered, they would be miserable.

Mercuries are useful in so many ways that it's a surprise when they resent their own utility. They're usually first to volunteer for a project, and quick to offer their opinions. Mercuries delight you by anticipating your needs. They arrange activities, recruit participants, and entertain everyone effortlessly; you'd think they'd be proud of the service. But their fantasies revolve around pulling strings, not being pulled.

Saturns and Jovials make a Mercury nervous. He assumes the Saturn is there to look over his shoulder, and is going to limit his field of activity. He suspects the Jovial is humoring him. Either is disconcerting, but not nearly as much as being ignored; it's the only action he can't forgive. It's better to find some way to communicate with him, even if it's caustic, because if you disregard him or his concerns you are going to make an enemy. Then he'll get your attention for sure.

Entertaining is natural for Mercuries, and they're electric in company, working the crowd, sincere and

MERCURIAL

confidential no matter whom they're talking to. They love to correct you, but aren't actually interested in hanging around for the conversation to ripen; they never have time with so many people to see. They relish dressing up, and frequently appear in what looks like a costume. They use these costumes to create dramatic entrances and exits, and as disguises to obscure their plans, their intents, or their identity. You'll often see Mercurial men sporting a neat moustache or beard which not only adds to the show but helps them overcome that embarrassing young look they maintain even late into life.

A Mercury's youthfulness announces itself in many ways. He looks the youngest of all the types and his age may surprise you. Although he's in a rush to grow up, and has an adolescent's prickly sensitivity to anyone who doesn't take him quite seriously enough, the pranks, teasing, tantrums, and innocence of childhood never really leave him.

As children Mercuries are manipulative and precocious. Their sunny dispositions and passion for approval make them bright and ready to please. Sparkling eyes and a quick wit delight us, too, and their resonant voices can arouse us like no one else's can. They're fun to be with, and enjoy life at a trot.

Their thoughts race along at the same speed that their moods change. A spitting rage will descend on them in a moment, and then blow over like summer clouds, the day sunny again. A Mercury is an impulsive creature, rash and heady for action, ready to go and

69

itching with impatience at any delay. His attention flickers from one subject to the next, never lingering long before setting out on a new course. His restlessness comes from an overactive mind, and from the durability of his dissatisfaction.

These restless impulses compel Mercuries to take charge of projects with enthusiasm. They can often be found organizing, innovating, filling all sorts of active roles with confidence. Their activity is joined to a lithe masculinity. Mercuries are quite capable of sliding into a more passive role, and have no difficulty acting the victim. Their masculinity doesn't get in the way of their playing this role as long as there's an advantage to be gained, and Mercuries certainly have enough complaints to sustain it. Perhaps they'll get something through your sympathy, and they don't particularly care what tools it takes to get it.

Two of Shakespeare's most interesting villains shed light on the Mercurial type. Iago offers an extreme picture. All his weaknesses are blown to distortion, and all his strengths have been bent to evil ends. But in his jealousy and fear Iago reveals the mind of Mercury at its most scheming. His inner fire can only be used for his own advantage, or for revenge; he has no humanitarian motives, none that don't concern Iago. His wounded pride is so palpable that it has consumed its host, and almost become a character in its own right.

Shakespeare's other great Mercurial schemer is Cassius, whose "lean and hungry look" depicts a side of Mercury that's so common it's become a cliché. These characters portray not only a narrow self-interest, but the antipathy that exists between Mercury and Mars, the two active, negative body types. Iago and Othello, Cassius and Caesar, Mercury and Mars. All have an instinctive distrust. They are like flint and steel, or oil and water; they just don't mix. At the opposite poles of activity, when these two negatively-charged types rub each other, their chemistries explode. You can find them at war in myth, in fantasy, in art, and in literature, where the stealth of Mercury opposes the power of Mars.

Today's casting directors use this antipathy, and our instinctive reactions to it, in much the same way as the artists of the Renaissance used it to cast the models in their paintings. The cops in our movies are frequently Martial; honest, straight talkers who don't waste time being nice, and who achieve by their persistence what intuition, which they distrust, would arrive at in a leap.

Crooks and charmers are Mercurial; childish, shiny and too sharp to be honest. Tight shots show us their shifty eyes. This is the giveaway that lets us see through their disguise in a moment, and clues us as to who's the villain.

The ultimate in disguise comes from the combination of Venus and Mercury. Together these types can produce a chameleon who is compelled to obscure his own identity, one who has the ability to go unnoticed by others. The warmth of Venus can also temper the hard edges of Mercury, and give the quicksilver, changeable type a base in the earthy, sensuous world. But because the world of nature is—in its activity—amoral, Venus adds nothing to the sporadic, or opportune, morality of Mercury.

The life I'm describing cannot be an easy one. Mercuries are besieged by energy that their body can't handle. They develop nervous tics and awkward mannerisms. They expect betrayal and, finding it everywhere, grow callous. They have trouble baring their emotional life, and think themselves shallow. Their occasional flare-ups surprise more moderate types. Role-playing eases their way in society, but also keeps an undercurrent of discomfort alive; watching the effects that their acting has, they are alternately bemused and baffled by their audience.

Mercury is redeemed by its perception, wit and humor. The speed of their intellect gobbles facts and stores reams of scripts. They can be smooth talkers or inspired orators, hell raisers or symbols for an aroused citizenry. We prize them for their bright air and their facile friendship. Mercuries amuse and entertain us as no other type can. They lift the clouds of our dullness and sweep us out of our doldrums. Even if it's only for a few minutes, we seem to fly into a finer air, and the electricity and brightness of their attention makes us, at those moments, giddy with life.

SATURN

MODERATION RULES the Saturnine world, whose inhabitants pay homage to it with prayers of restraint and self-denial. In this world spontaneity counts for little, unpredictability is a cardinal sin, and the righteous path is the one that seems safest. It is a world of cool, correct rationality, a world logically ordered and precisely planned.

Reflected in the facets of every Saturn's life is a sweeping, panoramic view. They gather for their knowledge a broad mix of facts, and organize them into a beautiful structure. Into this structure they fit new details as the need arises; they don't tamper with the edifice itself. Each fact bears weight, and each is treated equally. It's the orderly accumulation that Saturns admire, and that entrances them. The view they get of life tinges their relations with the other types, and gets ineradicably fixed.

Saturns approach each day as an opportunity to enhance the program of existence that they've concocted. Steady progress supplies the real joy they get from experiences, and gives them all the meaning they need. It leads them to arrange their lives in copious detail. They can start their list for the day with an instruction to themselves to "wake up". Why should any moment be unaccounted for? An unplanned day looks to a Saturn the way a mine field looks to a soldier about to cross it; like chaos, where anything may happen, and he's compelled to prepare for it.

But he can accept help only on certain conditions. He would like you to remember the balance in his thinking. He would like you to realize that he will understand your information better than you do yourself, even while you're telling him where the mines are. He'll act the judge with you, and in a pose of judicial concentration will listen to your advice, nodding to himself as testimony proceeds. He's allowed you to say your piece, and will notify you later of his decision.

Hierarchy is a natural product of all this orderly thinking. It's the translation into the language of human interactions that comes most easily to Saturns. They want to know their place, and your place, in detail. They're interested in every measure of control and every line of authority that might affect them. Titles, credentials, and qualifications give them a smooth method for classifying everyone, proofs of competence and approval that they can trust. It makes the hierarchy go.

Saturns move seriously, behave seriously, and play seriously. Their gravity adds force to their character, and warns off the lighthearted. They aren't amused by your foolishness, but will record it as judiciously as any other bit of information they come across. A Saturn is serious because he assumes life is serious; he can't see it any other way. Besides, without his gravity what good would all his regimens and disciplines be? At any moment decisions may have to be made, or an action may be called for. How will he know what's right? He'll have to consider closely . . .

Saturns are taller than most people, and tower over the other types. They find an advantage in their height; it's simpler to dominate someone who must look up to you. Saturns have an aristocratic air; their measured pace, thoughts of social elevation, and scrupulous fairness assure them a place in society. They rise like cream in all sorts of organizations, and find themselves managing companies, clubs, or countries as chairmen, administrators, or presidents.

It was some antique Saturn, I'm sure, who devised the art of delegating. This democratic way of work allows a department to excel if everyone does what he's been asked to do, assuming the overall strategy is sound. Of course, it's usually a Saturn who's doing the asking. He has the only copy of the complete plan, and you get the morsel he thinks you need to get your particular job done and no more.

Predictable things comfort Saturns. I had a friend staying with me who confessed to this. He said his day could only start on a harmonious note if his breakfast were properly controlled. Each morning I'd find him at his meal, alone, with a plain white bowl he'd brought with him set squarely on the table. He was eating one of those cereals that gleefully substitute nutrition for flavor, and which he had also brought along. His spoon lay perpendicular to him on the table, polished and packed for just this purpose. The importance he assigned to each tool was indicated by its position in the ritual. Needless to say, he had some internal bell that signalled the start of this monastic banquet at the same moment each day.

Like Venusians, Saturns are at home with what seems safe. I've seen Saturns who, finding a restaurant they like in a new city, dine there every night for a week. Why aren't they drawn to variety like most of us? Their need for constancy is stronger, that's all. They'll sacrifice all the untasted novelties on the menu for the guaranteed pleasure of the prime rib they had last night.

For the same reason Saturns are insincere gamblers. Inching ahead on safe bets, they'll never shoot the works, or strive for that rush of abandon that lifts you when the odds get so steep you have to believe in magic to put your money down. They stick with their system instead, intent on the "sure thing".

Here's a type that routinely denies itself. Saturns sometimes seem reason's revenge on humanity; their spontaneity has been leached out, leaving them phlegmatic and a bit gray. They don't leap to opportunity, but carefully work out the pros and cons of every situation. They plan in order to avoid the pitfalls of life rather than to take advantage of its pleasures. A well-charted itinerary can make their hearts beat quick.

These people love the power of facts. A Saturn is sure that through facts he can prove his precision, his decisions, and his rational muscle. He'll weigh all sides of a question and hope to come to some ultimate certainty. Nevertheless, he can just as easily lock himself in indecision when he gets the awful feeling that he might have to act before all the facts are in. So he'll spend hours mulling over what he knows, and rehearse the ramifications of all sorts of improbable events. But he's having a Saturnine version of fun while he's at it.

It's no wonder Saturns like to count everything. They measure, judge, and compare madly, generating points for further consideration. This is especially true for anything that can be calculated. Numbers seem ruthless to them, incontestable, and free of messy uncertainty. Emotion, passion, and unreasonable desires have no place in calculations, and are left out. This classifying ardor, putting everything in its proper place, inspires Saturns throughout their lives.

We're living in a *Saturnine* era—we think almost anything of value must be measurable, and anything we can measure must be of value. What's your IQ? How cold is it? Wind chill? Degree days? Rank of a tennis pro? Percent first serves, faults, unforced errors, record against under-21 year old left-handed players in rain on clay during June? New restaurant? Two stars, four forks, and three dollar signs. Who's getting into Harvard this year? Combine the SAT's with the scores awarded for drive, connections and ambition and you'll know. Yes, it's everywhere.

With Saturn running wild, we're less sure of many things than we think we ought to be. Too many experiences don't answer to reason, and all our rationale hasn't made us more nimble when it comes to dealing with the unpredictable. At some point we come to learn the limitations of our own logic and the methods it's tried to impress on us. We look for new ways to understand, link them to our logical abilities, and hope the combination creates a more powerful tool.

Saturns require a good deal of time to discover this, and some never do. The dream of complete predictability never dies for them. Having confined their thoughts and plans within the rigid structures of hierarchy and priority, they get trapped there, and can't find the way out. For these people form, rule, and ritual assume the aspects of grace itself. Nebulous, messy, or overly emotional experiences are replaced with a safe repetition of movements, meetings, and sacraments that satisfy all their needs much more cleanly.

Symmetry in design will please a Saturn, like the visual balancing you see in the works of the Flemish painter Jan van Eyck. These pictures always look to me like the result of a well-worked math problem. It's a type of display which pleases a Saturn exactly because it demonstrates its own internal order so forcefully. Stating the problem and showing its solution reinforce his commitment to structure and logic. He feels that to veer away from these principles will bring danger in the form of unpredictability looming on every side.

Saturn is the type of regimentation and rule, law

and legislation, and all the agreements we reach at various levels of society that allow us to live together. Their concern for equality and their literal interpretation of laws make Saturns great champions of the persecuted, including those who've been let down by their systems. Many are avid and selfless workers for social justice. They are the Saturns whose reasoning about life happened to have grown into an idealistic, rather than a selfish, mold.

The mature Saturn at work is a wonder to behold. He goes from dawn to dusk no matter how dry or menial his task, and slakes his thirst with measured sips of water. It isn't as difficult for a Saturn to deny himself little pleasures this way as it would be for you or me. It's a conscious suppression of desires in favor of what his mind has told him is the reasonable route to his eventual aim.

A Saturn seems more cut off from his own emotions and sensations than other people. His heavy, serious face falls into a neutral expression when you're talking, as if deciding which response he's going to allow himself. This look also lets you know he's not enslaved by any of them. Saturns must be wired differently than other people. Maybe they have a switch that can be thrown to short-circuit the messages of pain or passion that would otherwise race from their minds—a neat trick that leaves them free to follow the plan of the day.

It's not surprising that a Saturn is most comfortable by himself, or with a fellow Saturn who can contribute independent teamwork, someone willing to work on a cooperative plan. In part, he isolates himself because he can't find anyone with the same standards of objectivity and decorum.

When he's with other people he's instructing them. He has advice to offer if you're buying tires, or having a baby. Whether he owns a car or has a family himself doesn't matter. He's convinced he can think about your concerns better than you can, and he doesn't understand why you put so little value on his recommendations. Because he's protective, and because we fall so easily into error, this responsibility may be a burden, but it's one he can't ignore.

People thrive within Saturn's paternal atmosphere, and in a circle of friends it's likely to be a Saturn who finds himself cast in the role of counsellor, or confessor. Where Mercuries always look for the opportunity to act, and feel the stage constantly calling to them, Saturns wait for an opportunity to make subtle but important distinctions, and to point to a correct course of action. They want you to call on them to decide, to render an opinion, and when you petition a Saturn for guidance, he slips effortlessly into the role of the judge.

Nothing fits a Saturn's didactic nature so well as the prospect of being called on to arbitrate, to adjudicate, to distribute his wisdom and comprehension. This is his chance to educate you in the details of your own self-interest. He knows in every case what you should do, and what you shouldn't. If you're foolish enough to ignore his advice, he'll shake his head, and wash his hands of the disaster you're about to bring on yourself.

He will wear the judge's robes he's donned whenever possible. He doesn't like to get involved in parochial fights, like the ones we have with a neighbor or competitor. Instead he waits for the chance to introduce his diplomacy, and is always available as a referee or a teacher. He wants you to make use of his sense of discernment. If he's allowed to rule unmolested, he'll be on hand.

Father wields the rod at home, and Saturn is the authority for the house of types. But nothing is sacred in his schemes. He'll sacrifice what seem to be our most human drives in favor of the rules of a regimen he's invented. And once he gets going on one of his homemade programs, every part of his life can be called into question, analyzed, and regimented.

For example, he'll program his sex life like a self-prescribing marriage counsellor. Two nights a week, with a progress report on the agenda for the third night. Saturns see nothing unusual about premeditation like this that might stifle others. But with Saturn, everything's a program. He eats an orange for the vitamin C; if it tastes good, that's a plus. Don't assume he's even noticed.

There's a mind like a sphinx in Saturns; their mental gaze seems permanently fixed on some far horizon. They leave us with the feeling that their ruminations are beyond our scope. The picture that we have of an absent-minded professor, bumbling in the details of life while his mind soars through abstract spheres, is one picture of Saturn.

Some Saturns are eccentric loners, absorbed in themselves, who go glassy when you mention the plumbing. Gaskets and joints have no place in their dreams of order and systematic action. Only the abstract, the theoretical, and the planned are perfect enough to satisfy them. They get no bite out of life. It has none of the sting, none of the bittersweet pain that turns to pleasure, none of the blooming sensuality of life that exists only for itself, the way a hand moving over a lover's body exists only for itself.

They don't hit for the brute pleasure of contact, or gorge themselves, or pick a fight, or drink too much. On the other hand, you can't feel sorry for Saturns because the tempo and tone of their lives obviously please them so much.

Saturns are drawn to philosophy and history, where their accumulation of facts has a noble tradition and their breadth of view has ample room to roam. We admire philosophy and history for just this reason, too, that they lift our own thoughts from the thicket of life and give us, for a moment, a more spacious view. It's a view that Saturns embrace, and over which their minds sweep in a ceaseless search for patterns that can be made to conform to Saturnine principles of thought and action.

Looking over a corporation of which he is the head, a Saturn will try to find those large shifts of manpower and resources that will better organize or more efficiently produce the work of the company. Scanning the movements of history, he will try to find the generalities that are always true, the rules that guide the forces in events. From this he propounds a theory.

The broad view, the historical perspective, make a Saturn moderate and discreet. Putting things in perspective separates him from more immediate feelings, and he becomes aloof, detached. His concerns sweep over forces that move masses of people. These forces are so much larger than any individual that we sometimes wonder whether a Saturn can see those around him as friends, colleagues, or lovers, and not just as historical units.

While a Saturn may be interested in humanity, he is just as capable of withdrawing from society. Saturns want to save you and guide you to truth because it's their mission, but with all their seriousness they don't come off well at parties. Their gravity points up our foolishness, suffuses us with a vague guilt, and cools our wit. They remind us of the teachers, priests and parents whose influence still lurks inside us. They add weight to all our thoughts, and pull from many people a long sigh of melancholy sobriety.

I suppose it's this leavening effect, and their limited repertoire of expressions, that make us want to tease Saturns so much. We poke them, kid them, put them on, in the hope of getting some kind of reaction. We're challenged by the constancy of their demeanor, and want from them something more approachable than a cool judicious gaze.

Saturns are so serious that when we're in their company our choices of action are severely restricted. You can fall into their steady pace; you can fly into extreme and eccentric behavior out of frustration, or to change the tone; or you can leave. They are often in the same predicament. Without a group to dominate, a circle to educate, or a project to regulate, they're lost, and will soon find a corner in which they can patiently observe the oddities of humanity. Or they'll lose themselves in introspection. Perhaps they'll find another Saturn to share this moment with; at least another Saturn will understand.

Clumps of Saturns, like groves of trees, don't fidget or jump; the slow whisperings of their conversation are punctuated by slow pauses for reflection. They don't use their hands very much when they speak, marking only a crucial point here or there with a calculated gesture. Their height alone would set them apart, but combined with the formality of their movements and the equanimity of their mien, their height ensures that they'll always be noticed.

Saturns are just too decorous a type to be much fun. Too concerned with the right word, the best school, the appropriate remark. They're not going to sacrifice all their work for the sake of an impulse. And nothing is more unnerving than a Saturn, awkward and stiff, trying to be spontaneous because someone's told them to loosen up. You know instinctively they'll never succeed, and are grateful to see them restored to their propriety when the experiment's over.

A faculty for mental organization gives Saturns an intuitive grasp on how things are structured, how things

84

work. From this sense spring their most constructive achievements. They can ignore their own desires to advance their plan, or the plan they've agreed to. It's his principles that compel a Saturn to carry each project to its completion.

His zest for structure and form may slip into dogma, and then he'll only be satisfied by strict rules and rigid procedures. His thinking gels in a fixed pattern, and the form of a ritual can acquire more meaning than what the ritual was designed to accomplish. Meetings are held because they've been scheduled, whether there is business to transact or not.

Moderation reigns and the mean becomes the road to salvation. Saturns set aims to an agenda. They carry them out with a deliberate, measured step, and track their progress on notebooks, calendars, and checklists. We may not fathom what joy Saturns get from all this until we understand that for them the joy is in the doing—often in simply getting things done.

Dogmatism of this sort can ruin a Saturn's efforts. The yearning for a great scope of understanding then crowds out the time it would take to penetrate any one study in depth. The search for objectivity may cause him to lean heavily on formulas; an arrangement of ideas that will always be true.

He may start to demand that everything fit his way of thinking, and discard the dynamic energy of contradiction. The tension that irreconcilable ideas give off can be cast aside in favor of neatness. The symmetrical solution must be the right one, no matter how synthetic.

He gets mesmerized with order, and may be tempted to seal off the chaotic sides of his own nature, the very wrinkles that could relieve his greyness and add a little color to his comprehension.

But Saturns provide us with balance and care. At their height, the moderation, discipline, and justice of Saturns come together to remind us of the nobility that lies in mortal men. The wisdom of Saturns speaks of some higher level of thought and action, that elevation of our highest potentials in which order, wrestled from the chaos of this world, is transformed into a divine harmony.

MARTIAL

MARS IS AN ACTIVE, NEGATIVE TYPE whose influence courses through the enneagram at the last flood of the development of masculinity. The stoical manliness of Saturn is intensified in Mars until it explodes in action, before fading into Jovial.

Mars is violent, but it can be effective. It is energy in its purest and most indiscriminate form. In this type power comes to its fullest force; Martials hum with it. Energy floods the spirit of a Martial and overflows into everything he does. For a Martial, whether at the head of an army marching for war, or desperately wrestling with his inner demons, it's the energy of his actions on which he is drunk.

A Martial's compact, powerful body and vivid, freckled complexion herald his arrival. Red hair waving and a determined look in place, he strides right up and crashes through whatever conversation you happened to be having. He thrusts his barrel chest out as far as his chin, and spreads his legs in a firm and ready stance.

Everything he's concerned with has an urgency and

just won't wait. If you don't acknowledge him, or if you try to finish your talk, the muscles in his neck bulge and perspiration covers his forehead as he tries to stare you into submission. If you don't give in to his bullying, he'll stomp off irate and disgusted, and mark you for a fool.

There's something in a Martial that won't let him live without a goal. Since he works from a plan, with specific points to be passed, he finds a well-defined aim the most practical approach. Mostly, he believes in what he can see, and not much more. Simple concepts are all that are required to connect him with his team, his school, or his country, and to give him a place to hang the pennants of his loyalty and fierce pride. He will work towards an aim in common with others if the work he's asked to do supplies him with visible, practical results. And he frets deliciously until his job is done.

Martials don't know how to pass an aimless life, or even an aimless day. To those of us who are more passive, or more changeable, who enjoy an unplanned ramble through a new city, or who can shrug off the tour we've scheduled in favor of a few magical hours loitering in a street-side cafe, to all of us, Martials look obsessed.

A Martial can become a man unable to live without something to do, something to be working on; he can be tyrannized by his own ceaseless drives. His aims and plans can squeeze him into a life of measured progress and undeflected, joyless striving. Or they can send him thrusting and crashing through his days, pursuing one credential or achievement after another.

Ferocity, loyalty, and vitality, the hallmarks of the consummate military man, are also the marks of this body type. Martials' minds and bodies naturally snap into military postures, which accounts for their disciplined attitudes. It's a posture, a way of approaching life, that seeps into their thinking, eating, sleeping, dressing, driving, talking, loving, and dying.

They have the wariness of the professional soldier at the front, and his feisty abandon at play. Martial men like to go carousing, and drink themselves into a stupor. Martial women grow out of their tomboy childhood, and go on to become athletic and competitive achievers, pioneering new roles for women.

Going on vacation with a Martial may make you think you're on a military campaign. He knows intuitively that surprise will be of decisive advantage in the plan of battle he's formulating. Lightning attacks on museums and other temples of culture reveal the strategy he's gleaned from this realization.

He manages to take yards of paintings hostage, captures acres of sculpture with a quick look. His pace never flags. Are there eight sights on the day's itinerary? The order of battle is drawn. Maximum use of transport, supplies, and resources is planned. Precise allowance is made for efficient utilization of time at each target. It's a bit of astute planning he thoroughly enjoys.

Hotel is base camp where maps and guides are assembled. The real fun of logistics, timing and fallback positions comes next, because Martials are very realistic about all the things that can go wrong and foul their plans. Step by step the Martial proceeds, and each completed segment of the day is a victory. He gets his joy from checking off the stages of his progress, from the visible confirmation that he's done what he set out to do.

This regimented world is infused with the air of latent power. Martials are warriors, and the logic of the battlefield never completely leaves them. A Martial relies on his friends as does the soldier on his foxhole buddies, but even then he may require that you prove your affection or demonstrate your loyalty before you convince him of your sincerity.

The first thing a Martial wants to know about you is simple; are you a friend or a foe? If you tell him you're neutral, he thinks it's a trick, that you're feinting, or that you're hiding your true feelings. He can admit that he's not sure of some people's loyalties, but it's a strain on his ethics. He can't be comfortable with people who won't take a stand, and he won't know how to act with you until he finds out onto which side of the fence you're going to fall.

Above all Martials value direct and simple speech, which they understand as easily as they do direct and simple action. They rely on people to mean what they say, and are impressed by a blunt truth no matter how painful it is for them to hear it. Martials expend their energy on the crises which litter their lives, and which make everything troublesome and wearying. The intensity it takes to keep putting out fires gives them the added pleasure of an excuse to subordinate their own interests and comforts in order to deal with the prevailing emergency.

If we admire Saturns for their counsel, and Venusians for their warmth, we admire Martials for their vitality. When you need something done, it's a Martial that you want to have on call. He can slash red tape, fire a stalled project, and plow through maddening detail. He'll rake your yard, re-do your den, and hang your pictures—faster than you can. He knows the perfect time to do whatever needs to be done: *now*. These people are designed for action. They get their results not because they can do so much, but because they never stop until the job's done.

Brimming with intensity, a Martial burns his volatile fuel driving through activities, and when he gets keyed up, he's fierce. Once he's touched by something he accelerates quickly through his emotions, and soon arrives at a peak of agitation. Whether he's revelling at his local pub, or beginning to steam at some politician, he comes to a head in a minute, and stays there until his energy's spent.

For a Martial, infatuation turns to obsession in an instant. Then he dashes into an affair, becomes the ardent lover, and may spontaneously fly halfway around the world in hot pursuit of the latest object of his desires. The scent of conquest dizzies him; his focus narrows, he won't swerve from his hunt, he never listens to reason, and he may well become unstoppable.

Martials live in extremes, and are drawn to the rough edges of life, where things seem more exciting.

They can be civil and well-behaved at the office, but when there's no hint of danger or controversy, they're only half-alive. Their restlessness is a constant. It doesn't leave them whether they're mowing the lawn or wrestling a sculpture from stone. There's a force behind their actions, and a heat that burns through obstacles.

Martials don't mind finding themselves in a tight corner; it justifies the ruthlessness that will be necessary to get out of it. And although they're usually open about their plans, don't think they're always being honest, or that they're incapable of a strategic deception once in a while. Their strength lies in the unspoken commitment they've made to themselves: to overcome whatever is blocking their way. It gives them a reason to exploit all of their resources, to hold nothing back.

Martials regularly appear in the front ranks of protest marches, hunger strikes, and political rebellions. They chafe at negotiations, and would rather test their power face to face against their opponents'. They are the firebrands and revolutionaries, inflamed and loyal to a cause, who are out to stir up the populace. They seem doomed to be always in opposition, and their rebellious nature eventually gets them in trouble. After the fight's been fought they'll be on the outside again, smoothly replaced by more manageable types.

Martials are impatient with long-term settlements, won't stand any nick in their principles, and think that social change will sooth the itch they've got. They seem naïve to someone less literal, as if they were unprepared to deal with people who know how to hide their motives.

92

Most of our views of Martials show them restless and in motion. It's rare to find one in repose, because when he's not absorbed in work, he's working out. You'll see him jogging in the morning, pacing in his office, and squirming at the opera. He always seems to be on the move, dashing across town or trekking in Tibet. He's comfortable outdoors, where his pioneer spirit and his thirst for freedom of action can run unchecked.

One source of a Martial's pride is his self-reliance. He considers himself the best choice for most projects, and doesn't see how anyone else could possibly do as good a job. He would rather build his house himself, without anyone else to slow him down. If you offer to help, he'll probably refuse because he sees you as an obstacle, and wants to be left to follow his own frenzied pace.

He insists on his independence, and values others who seem as self-sufficient as he. A Martial thinks people who surround themselves with friends, or who find plenty of acquaintances to chat away the hours with, are weak. But he gets frustrated with himself when his bluntness—or his barroom humor—drives others away.

Small talk unsettles Martials. Banter bores them unless it's got an edge, or shows signs of escalating into an argument. They love to find a flaw in your reasoning, and hope you'll take their attack as the chance for a brawl. Then a Martial really comes alive. Zeroing in on you like a pilot screaming down on a bombing run, he finds the crack in your defenses, and drops his load. He'll rarely miss an opportunity to attack, and expects

93

you to fight back. But if you try attacking him first, he takes your criticism too hard, and sulks away convinced he's been treated unfairly.

If you're looking for Mars, look for the frontal assault, the provocative remark, the direct opposition. Behind them you'll find a Martial, itching for a fight. He's blunt, and tries to shock you. He'll adopt a rigid moral stand, or a purposefully crude tone to get your attention, or to get you mad; it's the same to him. He gets a thrill from opposing you no matter what you've said, and hammers away just to test your fortitude.

When he's riled, you can't deal with a Martial. If you say he's being unreasonable, that everything is ambiguous and life is full of contradictions, he presumes you're feeble. He's taken a stand on principle, and won't be budged. He demands that you take a stand too, and goads you with his brutal logic and insinuations of weakness until you either stand up and fight or walk away.

Oddly enough, he doesn't want to convert you to his position, because then he'll always distrust your commitment. Martials want loyalty from us, or they don't want us at all: *America, love it or leave it! My country, right or wrong!* Although he may think your ideas are mistaken, nothing will rouse his scorn so much as your deserting those same ideas.

A Martial swings his spade at intruding weeds in the garden with the same resolute violence which, in another age, he used to swing his awful sword at rows of his enemies. He knows only one way to do things:

94

with vigor. Compromise is a sin to him, and diplomacy the habit of lying about your own feelings. He has little use for subtleties, which leave him frustrated. The explanations he appreciates are short and to the point.

I used to live with a Martial who always gave me the impression that she was engaged on a great commission, no matter how ordinary her errand turned out to be. Her footsteps echoed throughout our house, beating a cadence of resolve and determination, even if she was only collecting the mail. I could tell what room she was in, and in what direction she was headed, and never feared that I wouldn't know when she'd arrived home or was going out. The vigor with which this woman washed dishes, the bang of the pots, the slam of the doors, echoed the vigor of her walk.

Martials are no good for stealth or covert manipulations. They would always rather tell you what they think, and take the consequences. They distrust Mercuries with a primal fervor, and if they find themselves in the same room with one, every muscle in their body can bristle with irritation.

A Venusian, however, is the ideal mate for a Martial. In a Venusian's lush passivity he finds a home for all his raging potency, no matter how rough it becomes. His energy thrills and enlivens a Venusian, who in turn evokes the Martial's more intimate feelings by appeals to his sensuality and protectiveness.

As long as a Martial isn't put off by Venus' apathy and passivity, this connection of types creates relationships, marriages, and affairs of great passion. Martials can be gentle with their children, but they also mix rigorous discipline and harsh expectations into their education.

Sexual vigor runs through Mars as potently as physical vigor does, and the type glows with it. Sex is one of the constants in the programs Martials have devised to reduce tension; they have an instinctive sense that sexual frustration can make them explode. They need sexual release more than anyone else, and without it may drop into an unfriendly funk. The sexuality in Martials, combined with both their physical vigor and their explosive temper, produces a nature more inclined toward violence than any other type. They simply have too much energy for the demands that life puts on them.

Although this is the same energy that fuels their ambition and drive, it also punishes their bodies. You'll notice a Martial grinding his teeth, bulging his neck, and tensing his back so habitually that if you try to give him a massage, his body feels like wood or steel, not flesh and blood.

With all this tension and energy surging through them, it's not surprising that Martials overdo things a bit. A Martial goes at life like one of those practitioners of karate—a *martial* art—who takes our breath away simply by trying to break taller, more unlikely stacks of bricks each time he swings. Martials get high on the scent of danger, and feed their addiction by driving too fast, hanging out of tall windows, or learning sky diving—where they get the additional thrill of throwing themselves from an airplane.

You see Martials in California's Yosemite Valley, where they hang suspended a few thousand feet up a sheer granite wall. They are the ones riding dog sleds in the arctic wilds, enthusiasts and explorers, brutally overcoming one barrier after another. The concentration required for these feats turns them into juggernauts, and reminds me of the early Christian crusaders who marched for thousands of miles across countries filled with hostile forces, eyes fixed on Jerusalem.

Martials are out setting records while you and I are at the office. They're pioneering new territories, making the necessary sacrifice. They throw their comforts away like chains that had tied them down; now they can get something done. They play at games and sports when hurt, determined to not baby themselves. They're certain they can always force their bodies farther, disregard their doctors' advice, think medication is for the weak, and, having gone beyond their endurance, make their bodies pay the price.

Even at a cocktail party, watch a Martial on the terrace where, like everyone else, he's leaning against a railing. But the Martial's compelled to lean just a little farther out over the edge, thrilling himself with the rush that fear brings. He's heady on the lunatic brew that's boiling inside him. While one voice in his head is telling him to stop, another is urging him to jump; the adrenaline produced by this internal tug-of-war is one

97

of a Martial's favorite feelings. It gives him something to struggle against when life threatens to become boring.

This struggle is what a Martial is after; he's honing his resolve against it. Difficulties are his insurance that he won't go soft. When he is uncertain about the solution he's found to a problem at work, or the course his team should take, he bullies his fears and bashes his doubts, and just charges ahead. To succeed in this world, he thinks, is to rule by your own force and iron self-discipline.

Martials may be impatient with civility and routine, but they quickly grasp the attractions of modern business life. Here they find a strict hierarchy, with its comforting and concrete labels and rewards. They feel that if they locate the paths of power and spar nimbly enough, they'll have an objective measure of their success: dollars and cents. Martials flourish in sales, where the intoxication of the hunt unleashes the full force of their competitive drive.

Of course, they're not all mercenaries and pugilists, and many Martials have taken their considerable zeal into less bloody arts. The paintings of Vincent Van Gogh, for instance, illuminate the type, stunning us as they do with their unconventional and perceptive vitality. Forms roil across Van Gogh's canvases, where he's traded delicacy for a demonic intensity. We can feel him caught in the grip of a great urgency, almost too piercing to bear. Yet he's channeled the violent energy of Mars within his own vision.

Ludwig van Beethoven, who outraged his contemporaries with his lusty and revolutionary music, demonstrates another side of Martial. He played the piano with an intensity that made the instrument jerk across the salon floor, and achieved heights of musical invention and dramatic effect despite the obstacles that dogged his days.

Martials are a pugnacious and feisty bunch, but I see their shortcomings most clearly in their need for difficulties. Hardships vivify them. Their insatiable drive gives them little leisure, but alerts them to potential disasters everywhere. They can't stop worrying the blemishes in their lives, and only want a chance to wrestle one-on-one with the demons they find there. They're sure that problems are coming around every corner every day, and get themselves so geared up for battle that they can't go through a supermarket, or wash the car, without throwing off at least a hint of frenzy.

It's remarkable, in a way, that the native skepticism of Mars doesn't poison their drive more than it does. Although a Martial can sink into a gloomy and rancorous depression, it's only a new challenge he's waiting for. When the resistance of a difficult project, a tough game, or an unexpected setback appears he puts away his misgivings and his fears, buffs up his persistent energy, and sets off to reach the goal on which his determined eyes have happened to alight.

JOVIAL

JOVIAL IS A STRANGELY ACTIVE type. After all, Jupiter is the first of the three passive types, but Jovials don't keep apart, like Lunars, or vegetate, like Venusians. Maybe it's the residue of activity from Mars that seeps into Jovials and makes them fling themselves into projects so intensely, makes them strive so energetically for the very depths of understanding.

When you see how a Jovial gets flushed by his latest enthusiasm, how he immerses himself in his subject, how he yearns to know every fact and name connected with it, how he airs his discoveries to all his friends, and how he draws many of these friends into his excitement, it's hard to remember that Jovial is a passive type.

But in Jupiter this is an on-again, off-again enthusiasm. They may be excited today about their latest cause, but don't bet that next week they won't be on a new diet, in a new sport, or studying art instead of selling stock.

Unable to resist the new, Jovials live a life of flux. They smell in novelty the giddy aroma of change, and succumb to it again and again. They get no solace from routine; it's routine that makes them itchy to move, that makes them long to ride the swell of something entirely new.

Cycling from peaks of enthusiasm through valleys of boredom, Jovials may accomplish little. They don't penetrate far enough, don't last through the rough spots that only discipline and persistence might help them with, before their interest has faded and gone.

This is a colorful type, even outrageous. A St. Nicholas type sometimes, but usually with round faces, round cheeks, and round shoulders, to go with their rounded outlook on life. Jovial men grow dewy with femininity when they're near Lunar, but Mars firms and intensifies them. Their hair falls out faster than their paunch expands, but not too much faster. The concert hall audiences and the musicians playing for them both display a high percentage of glittery Jovial heads; maybe it's the creativity inherent in their type.

Jovials like to make a splash in society, and use all their theatrical ploys to get themselves noticed. They heighten their dramatic entrances by the extravagance and range of their wardrobes. Their closets are stuffed with clothes which will become the costumes for the many roles a Jovial has to play. They're likely to have a variety of sizes on hand as well, confident that their fleshy bodies will continue to rhythmically expand and contract.

A Jovial's sweeping exits are just as impressive. He flings kisses and calls in all directions, throws his coat around his ample body, and all in all uses the drama and volume of his departure to leave the most vivid impression behind. He's always on stage.

The Dutch painter Rembrandt van Rijn was a fully-fledged Jovial, who painted himself and his models in the most fantastic and exotic costumes. This translation of his Joviality into his art is natural, and doesn't surprise us. Even a Dutch fishmonger in one of his paintings, loaded down under the opulent robes of some Turkish potentate, doesn't make us flinch.

Many novelties crossed Rembrandt's path. He lived in Amsterdam, the hub of a trading empire where all the fruits of trader nations were brought by the sailors and merchants amongst the seventeenth-century Dutch. He had so little resistance to these strange treasures that he eventually bankrupted himself and left the auctioneers costumes, gold helmets, Japanese armor and antique busts with which to pay his many creditors.

Yes, Jupiter is a prodigal type, wasteful and extravagant with money, lavish and reckless with promises. They provide so much entertainment for others, and so much succor, that we can't find it in us to hold their self-indulgence against them. A Jovial's parties attract just as many people when he's down and out as they do when he's thriving. He'll still feed you too much, make you laugh with his stories, and soothe your problems. Poverty doesn't force him to pull in the wings of his flamboyance; he lets it soar on credit instead.

This is a maternal type, fussy and caring. Its influence sometimes alternates with that of Saturn, a paternal type, and sometimes opposes it. Jovial finds a complement in childish and entertaining Mercury, and the attraction between these two is bright and electric. Together their wit flashes quick and keen, with a sharp and ready edge. They may also collapse into fits of bubbling hysteria that contort them both, and whoever else happens into their company, in spasms of laughter.

Mercury is really the perfect foil for Jovial. A Mercury's quick mind can keep up with a Jovial's circuitous reasoning, and Mercuries' hypochondria allows Jovials to indulge their need to nurture and care for others. Mercuries hunger for attention as voraciously as children do—a hunger that complements Jovials' need for students to lecture, to guide, and to counsel.

Like Mercuries, Jovials thrive in society. A Jovial loves to have people around, and as long as there isn't another Jovial to contend with, the more people there are, the better he'll like it.

People are the medium he lives in, the air he breathes. His address book bulges with the names of friends, associates, and acquaintances. He'll have the number of a stranger he struck up a conversation with on a train to London 12 years ago: But what an interesting person! If he happens to come across this name, he sets off on the tale—he thinks each of his stories is equally fascinating. Once launched, he doesn't need more than your nod to keep him going.

Jovials would like you to think that they only see the best in the people around them, but their gossip has a catty tone. They're committed to maintaining the bright and cheerful image they've got of themselves, and won't give up the stubborn optimism that makes it work. It's difficult to get helpful criticism from a Jovial, even when you want it. To criticize you pains him; either he's reluctant to hurt you with the truth, or afraid that he'll sacrifice his popularity by telling you something you didn't want to hear.

The fragility of a Jovial's self-esteem causes him to talk about other people in the rosiest terms. He's horrified by what might happen if he's honest and plain. He'll be affronted if you disagree with him, but he'll be mortified if you hint that you don't like him. Vanity makes him vulnerable to the manipulations of flattery and the humiliations of defeat. He thinks he's never wrong, or unlikable; according to all his evidence, Jovial is the *perfect* type.

This vanity can turn all his diamonds to dust. His easy prominence in social situations, the way he attracts people into his sphere of influence, everything that makes a Jovial popular, entertaining, or respected can turn against him. His vanity makes his humor into an ornament of his character. And while he can spot his friend's defects or his wife's obsessions as well as anyone can, his own conduct seems wonderful to him, his aims have true nobility, and his behavior borders on the sublime. He's likely to think: "I must certainly be a fine and entertaining fellow. Why else would all these nice people like me?'

Vanity pumps up a Jovial with ostentation, self-interest, and pomposity. Vanity inflates him with nervous confidence, behind which hides a delicate bubble of fear, a secret so fragile that it must be protected from the pinpricks of his own doubt. He refuses to accept the help offered by his friends, and thinks that loyalty means you'll never criticize him.

This folly distorts many of the talents of a Jovial. While he harmonizes the chords struck by each person around him into a fruitful and cooperative tune, it takes only one person who refuses to follow his score to drive him wild. He weaves insightful and amusing stories for an audience, but smothers any scent of competition under pillows of pointless verbosity, and ends up becoming a bore.

A Jovial may be a natural teacher, but he's the one you can't disagree with. He champions underdogs as long as they show their gratitude. He is an untiring organizer, insists on his firm sense of right and wrong, but he also wants to be sure you've spelled his name right on the program credits.

Yet by these devices a Jovial's vanity is thwarted and fails to reach its own goal. A Jovial feels that his faults blot his perfection, that his errors will drive people away. He may become pompous and evasive. But his friends wish he'd see his excesses the way they do, as pointing up his humanity, for which they would love him.

Jovials enjoy being teased and titillated; it revs their engine. They're after the spice in life, and want to take life in whole. Their appetites are pricked by curiosity, including their appetite for the new, the strange, and the odd. They collect stories of enigmatic characters, mementos of dramatic moments from their past, eccentric fragments of life. Their shelves overflow with the stuff, and they won't part with a penny of it; the chaos that results is a reminder of their travels, the wide range of their interests, how complex and multifaceted they must be. They live amidst a clutter of collectibles, and are comforted by them.

A Jovial is a kind and forgiving friend who welcomes you into his family. He'll loan you his car, find you a job, cook dinner for you, and slip you some cash to tide you over. He's ready to accept the responsibility for your happiness and well-being. He's distressed by the suffering of his friends or his family, or anyone else touched by his expansive feelings. He would like to help you through your times of difficulty and is willing to help you carry your burden as if it were his own.

It's hard for Jovials to fathom the utter randomness of disease and pain; the injustice of it defeats them. Their world, although colorful and varied, has more happy endings than ours does. Regardless of how low you've fallen, how desperate your circumstances look, or how dim your prospects seem to be, a Jovial will manage to find a silver lining to the cloud hanging over you. To pragmatic people, or those more cynical or ironic, Jovials simply seem unrealistic; the kind of people who are destined to be disappointed because they've never noticed that, in life, disasters are routine.

A Jovial remains a determined optimist about himself and his friends. He'll support your ambitions wholeheartedly, as long as you treat his advice with the gravity it deserves. If you wonder how to get his backing, try to determine the role into which he's cast himself. He may have decided to be your counselor, your teacher, your mother, or your guru. You run a risk if you step outside the role of the moment, and you may bring down on yourself the cruellest punishment that a Jovial can inflict on you—exile. He can't imagine anything more terrible than depriving you of his company.

This threat of exile is the sword a Jovial holds over your head, his punishment for bad behavior. Please him and all his caring attention is yours; disappoint him, and he'll cut you off completely, as if you'd never existed. His persuasions are all variations on a theme of debt and obligation. He lures you with promises of favor and corrects you by playing on your guilt.

Jovials seem to have a direct line to our fear of doing the wrong thing, which they systematically play on to keep us in line. If you can't step back from your desire to please people you may find yourself cast as a satellite to their star, and find it painful to disconnect from their influence.

A Jovial's power depends on his ability to arouse you, to move you, to make his vision seem like your vision. The sweep of his thinking and his flair for the dramatic enable him to convince you, if only for a moment, that parking his car, or stopping at the store, or whatever errand he's sent you on is one step in the march of human progress, and an honor he rarely bestows.

We're screened from the motives that may be driving a Jovial by the bluff and bluster that obscure his actions. Even his tact can get caught up in his manipulations. And it may never occur to us when we're involved in his call for selfless service that a Jovial's purpose may have a darker side which is just as hidden from him. He's become drunk on his own righteousness, and doesn't mind a little veiled seduction to get his way.

Jovials enjoy their capacity for pure power, the ease with which they control other people. They'll coerce co-workers or manipulate circumstances to earn an advantage. Aroused by a threat to their family or their prestige, they're ruthless.

But Jovials also get caught by the demands of their well defined self-portrait, in which they've painted an idealistic and utopian shape to their ambitions. They become experts at strategic omissions, and develop into elegant justifiers. They use all the art they can muster not simply to explain to you what they've done and why, but to reassure themselves at the same time.

An instinct for tact leads Jovials to success in diplomatic posts. Their commitment to harmony anchors their dedication to family, community, or country, in all of which they seek cohesion and balance. They may find themselves bringing opposing parties to a negotiating table, or arbitrating between warring friends. What they dispense is approval and support, not justice.

Rhetorical skills and personal magnetism launch Jovials into political life. They're well-suited to both trade and business, and may be chosen to run a company after they've demonstrated their competence and responsibility.

Being near a Jovial has a tonic effect on other people, and inspires their trust. The most reassuring and sympathetic doctors we meet are Jovials; somehow they not only share our pain, but make us feel they've helped our cure with a touch or a smile. They are the rare and sympathetic healers who are never too tired to stop by to see you, who always seem to have sweets in their pocket for any children they may come across.

Jovials have enough energy to support a small village of dependents, and surround themselves with cats, dogs, children, friends, family and colleagues. They love languages, and learn them readily. Their acting translates effortlessly to the stage, on which they can satisfy their craving for extreme behavior while getting heady with the prospect of fame.

Jovials like to spend money whether they have it or not; nothing will raise their spirits as fast as a little foray into conspicuous indulgence. They are neither humble about their talents nor discreet about their assets. They tickle themselves with the daring of their excesses; if you don't notice their diamond earrings, their alligator boots, or their new Chevrolet, what good are they? An abundance of cash gives Jovials a satisfied, well-fed look, as if they had earned the reward of self-indulgence.

A creative thread runs through some of this behavior. It glimmers in Jovials' constant re-imagining of themselves, the ongoing thrill of being on stage, the challenge of pure performance. It surfaces in their wit, and in the way their humor points out the contradictions and absurdities of life, yet leaves us gasping and holding our sides.

From Jovial farm girls aquiver with the synthetic lyrics of popular songs, to Jovial industrialists stirred by their collections of corporate art, even to the booming Jovial voice of Walt Whitman celebrating himself and the universe, people of this type find art and crowd it into their lives.

The life of a musician and music as a rest from life charm them equally. As parents and artists they are prolific. Johann Sebastian Bach, a Jovial who produced music all his life as easily as most of us breathe, fathered more than thirty little Bachs as well.

The history of art certainly isn't a strictly Jovial domain; it's much too human and too varied a pursuit, and one that has a place for every type. But crowding all around you'll find Jovials trying to satisfy the craving they've got for art in any form.

They become patrons of artists, art historians, curators, symphony supporters, opera fund-raisers, endowers of new museum wings, and friends of conductors. I'm not sure I've ever met a Jovial who didn't either write poetry, or read it. Without much perseverance, a Jovial flits from one experiment to another, makes a film one year, throws some pots the next, and always seems on the verge of signing up for yet another evening course that's struck his fickle fancy. Jovials are consummate dilettantes.

But all this art and eclecticism tells us something else about Jovials, something that's also reflected in the

110

cohesiveness they work on others. It tells us about a longing bred into them, that spreads throughout much of their thought and behavior; a longing for harmony.

When I say harmony, however, I mean that Jovials cast themselves as the harmonizing force. Mere order won't satisfy them, the kind that disciplines give you, or the order that flows from a strict sense of form. They're after something different; connections in meaning, not chronology.

Jovials want to understand everything in depth, they want to connect every fleeting feeling, every new thought, every second of experience, to every other feeling, thought and experience. They may have a map of the meaning of life, but it doesn't satisfy them. They want to strip it from the wall and wrap it around a globe, get an idea of the real relationships at work between things.

When they try to extract meaning from the tiniest scraps of experience, Jovials can sound absurd about as often as they seem profound. The distinction is one that matters little to a Jovial who's on a roll, audience in hand, casting his mind over wider and wider tracts of time in the search for connections, correspondences, explanations, and coincidences.

Some people think that this habit, which contributes so much to the part they play in society, is propelled by their craving for art. But to me it's a sign of that desire in Jovials that fuels not only their art but their lives; the desire to bring everyone they love, everything they know, to sound one all-inclusive chord. When for a moment they realize this aim they sweep us all along with them, and give us a glimpse of some high and illuminating harmony that lies behind our entire world.

SOLAR

SOLARS FASCINATE ME; they fascinate everyone who isn't Solar. They are as close as a human can come to passing from material flesh to pure energy. They are to the rest of us what a hummingbird is to robins, chickadees and chickens; the speed limit of the species. Solars, dashing and dancing about, can make you think their nerves are going to fray from overuse, or that their bones are about to fly apart.

Burning bright and intense, Solars are in constant motion. They dance when they walk, mime while they talk. Their eyes flicker from side to side when they're standing still, and gleam with intensity when you're talking to them. Energy animates their bodies and radiates all around them.

There's something strange about the Solar type, something off. It doesn't slip comfortably into the scheme of types; you've got to shoe-horn it in. It's a type that lacks the tensions of attraction and repulsion that inflame the other types. Their metabolism must be very different as well, to process fuel the way they do. Their differences are reflected in the enneagram we've used for plotting the course of the other types, but where Solar doesn't seem to occupy a distinct spot.

In some ways, Solar doesn't look like a distinct type at all, but more like a supercharger that can be fitted onto any of the other types. When you think you've seen a Solar, you've invariably seen other types in the person as well. Separating the Solar from what it's combined with can be difficult, and inconclusive. But the first signs of Solar, no matter where we find them, are excitement, excitation, energy, electricity, vibration, and just plain speed.

Lunar-Solars, Saturn-Solars, Venusian-Mercury-Solars, all the Solars are Solar-something, hyphenated types, people with built-in contradictions tugging at their varied, and sometimes incompatible, motives. And although we are all divided, unlike the impossibly pure types in this book, we can usually identify distinct strains of the basic types in ourselves. We can see each type's function, and try to organize these functions into a picture of our make-up.

In the study of Solar this process works differently. By being mated to other types Solar yields, for instance, a Jovial, but a revved up one. He's still Jovial, but he's been over-refined, drawn tight. Straight lines and sharp corners have replaced curves, bulges and mirth. This Jovial-Solar hybrid smarts easily because his vanity has been raised to a new level of excitation. He's become over-sensitive to criticism, and can't stop entertaining.

He's more captivating than an ordinary Jovial, but he's also more distant.

We need to know the traits of Solar to observe the type. But if we want to ferret Solar out, we also need to remember that these traits always combine with the traits of other types. When you look for Solars, look for them pure and undiluted; but look as well for the color they add to the types with which they combine.

People have odd ideas about Solar, partly because it's so difficult to keep your observation on two different things at once, in the way I've mentioned.

Some people will tell you that Solar appears in everybody's body type, no matter how small the dose. These observers measure Solar in parts-per-hundred with an apparently perfect gauge they've got in their minds. Other people claim to see nothing but a distinct type in Solar, one that doesn't mix. They treat Solars like unearthly children, in whose refinement lie the traces of a higher world. These people are awed by Solars, and aren't put off even when their favorites grow demanding.

It's better to be prudent, to go slowly. Get to know the six other types well, and keep Solar in the back of your mind, on call. It will explain many things you will see that you can't otherwise account for; it won't explain everything. If you're interested in learning types, then learn to wait for the recognition that snaps your head back, the shock you get when you really see a type.

The study of types demands that we keep our minds both open and cautious, and this is true nowhere more than in the study of Solar. Solars will enchant and beguile you, they will madden and may enrage you, but they will never bore you.

Solars energize us, even daze us. They make us come alive so we get filled with a nervous excitement. Solars don't seem to represent a particular function of ours, but rather heighten and extend our sensitivity to include a whole new range of impressions; we're quicker when we're around them. This energy accounts for most of the characteristics of Solar, and for the effects they have on everyone else.

Fair-skinned, with dark hair and wide-set, entrancing eyes, Solars vibrate more quickly than we do. They can charge the atmosphere around them with electricity and anticipation. Brilliant entertainers, they sail their act on a wave of intensity, and their energy carries us along for awhile. Solars have that quality of attraction, that personal magnetism some call *charisma*. We are drawn to them, but may not stay long; it's much too difficult to keep up with the rate at which they're burning, and with the flutter of their thoughts.

When they're active Solars are like children whose motives and morals have been transferred to the higher functions of an adult. They're restless, easily captivated, and changeable. They are on the verge of laughter, or about to swell into tears.

Solars yield to the same extreme emotions that children yield to, but with more force. Their tantrums are as teary as a child's, but more elegant. They want a toy

116

to make them feel better just as desperately, but the toy has become a mink coat.

Solars forget themselves the way children do; you have to remind them that it's cold outside, or they simply won't notice they were about to take a walk in a snowstorm without a coat. They skip meals without a thought, and when they become weak, attribute it to the exciting time they've been having. They are delicately made, susceptible to illnesses and ailments of many kinds. They seem as unprotected and unfinished as any of the other kids we know.

Like children, Solars delight in fantasy. But as adults, they can remain unaware of the brutality of life. They inhabit a black-and-white, good-or-evil world built like the world of fairy tales. Theirs is a romantic existence, sketched in simple tones. It's a world in which they know that awful dragons lurk in the dark woods, but never doubt that a young prince will reach his breathless, swooning princess just in time to save her.

Dreams maintain this romantic world. Disturbed by the random injustice and gratuitous violence of our world, Solars calm themselves with the dreams of their fantasies. They invest the world they've imagined with purity and goodness and, uplifted, overlook the harsh, the demeaning, and the bloody.

Solars create more than fantasies. Their creativity also emerges in plays, and in acting. It combines with their charisma to fashion them into singers and entertainers; you'll find them in all the worlds of make-

117

believe. They are poets of sensitivity, and artists with a delicate, rarefied vision.

Their active imagination clothes Solars in costumes designed to produce an effect, or to show which part they're playing today. They make a bright and bold impression in a group, their vibrant energy intensified by their habit of dressing in vibrant colors. They prefer an airy, ethereal look, or else a shocking one, and when they aren't looking frilly and feminine, they're likely to turn up in conspicuous combinations of red and black.

You can't help noticing Solars. The delicacy of their looks makes them stand out, and they take it naturally when they're cared for and admired. They're hothouse flowers that wilt without the heat of your attention, and think something must be wrong if you leave them even for a moment. They have no use for your criticism, constructive or otherwise; what they yearn for is your adoration.

Solars puzzle those of us who wonder why, since we're so easily captivated by them, they continue to seek out the crutch of our reassurance to prop themselves up. They glow with beauty and grace: Don't they know they're the objects of our envy? Or that we see in them the ideal prince or princess of the dreams left over from our childhood? But they crave approval with a hunger that can't be sated; they'll never cultivate what they need—self-assurance—from the junk food of our flattery.

You might say that Solars are too easily satisfied, that it's not a deep or penetrating understanding they're after, but a simplified one, a version they can repeat to themselves with conviction and assurance. The cut and color of a new dress is enough to inflame what seems their deepest feelings. It's in impressions, in the form and finish of a thing, that they get their thrills. If you become too serious, they sag. They'll wonder why you don't cheer up, and may not wait long for you to come around. Their lives are more fun with someone to play with.

You can see Solar women in clusters sometimes, twittering and feinting like high school ballerinas, all gawky limbs and hot-eyed looks. They're talking about shopping or, in certain circles, reciting fairy tales to each other in quivering tones, or telling the stories of their favorite operas.

Solar men are spare and wan, with high thrust foreheads and bright, feverish spots on opal cheeks. They're romantic poets, or dancers who jolt their audiences with electric leaps and searing glances. Matinee idols and cabaret singers, they throw magnificent rages, stamping their feet in bouts of pique.

No one else would trust some of the people that Solars attract. They put up no resistance to the people that crowd around them, and don't discriminate between the good advice they're given and the bad. As a result they're often victimized by seductive business managers, sleazy agents, and shyster lawyers.

An adolescent greed keeps pace with the rest of their personality and makes Solars sly and guarded. They get tense worrying about whether they'll get a fair

119

share. This is a tension that can make them intrusive, or rude. They think you should make exceptions for them, take their *differentness* into account. Don't you know they need special treatment, and that others are vying to take care of them?

Solars expect to ascend the social ladder, and don't mind the grasping involved to reach its successive rungs. At meals, even Solars who are quiet and tentative may attack their dinner mercilessly, dispatching great heaps of food to fuel their throbbing factory.

Solars practice a naïve control, trying to trick or charm you into helping them. Their attempts at persuasion, however, are often so obvious that you're as likely to be amused by them as irritated. We don't resent Solars for their intrigue or their success, and in spite of their impractical schemes they hold onto their many friends. Solars champion causes that go along with their rosy view of justice, and may select the victims they'll care for by picking the ones they think are the cutest.

Solars live an odd and fretful life, restless and frail, swept by the winds of their passions and the demands of their admirers. They rush hot and fragile through their days, and are liable to exhaust themselves early in life. They don't seem designed to last for a lifetime of toil, or built as if they were meant to attain any great age.

The highly colored, vibrant personalities of art and opera are frequently Solars. There's the brilliant Renaissance painter and colorist Raphael Sanzio, whose canvases combine the perfection of form and ethereal air we associate with this type. The extreme sensitivity and romanticism in the poetry of John Keats and Percy Shelley, their tragic lives and early deaths, all speak of Solar.

Then there's Giuseppe Verdi's tempestuous Violetta Valery of the opera *La Traviata*. As a character she exhibits all the traits of Solar. Violetta owns mesmerizing beauty and social wit. She has brilliant friends, engages in stormy affairs, and lives an opulent life given over entirely to play. The tragical action of the story hinges on her romantic abandon to a world of fantasy that eventually collides, as it must, with the requirements of an unjust and political world. At the end of the opera, it's her fragile constitution that sends her to an early, dramatic, and romantic, end.

A Solar is a positive type, which he demonstrates by his idealism and his optimism. He's active, which we can observe from his abundant energy. But unlike the other types, these characteristics don't limit the people he attracts, or the people to whom he's attracted. He works his magic on all the types, and appeals to us equally. Where we have been identifying active types with masculine energy and passive types to feminine, and finding in these relationships some clue to people's drives, in Solar we can't make the same connection.

This type doesn't seem to take a firm step in either a masculine or feminine direction. Instead, it adds to whatever type it's found with, but with unpredictable results. The Solar influence can make a woman vastly more airy, or shoot her through with ambition; is it masculine or feminine?

Solar rarely primes a man's virility. More often it induces a tremble, or vibrato into his chemistry that's unmistakably womanish. These men become poetic—and I mean too much so—and may lack the vigor it takes to engage in the manly arts of war or conquest. They don't belong in the arena, and their fragile health can undermine their drive for fame.

Solar inflames the metabolism of the people it affects, and produces a surplus of energy. But we can't take this energy and the activity it causes in Solars as masculine. A Solar's drive for sex can be intense, matching the intensity he produces in all his functions. He may find in sex an outlet for the excess energy his body produces, but at times he can also appear to be sexually neutral. Perhaps his attractions have more to do with excitability and a need for company than with the hungers of a Solar's body.

Solars spend a lot of time on their costumes, endlessly primping and preening. They log hundreds of hours in front of mirrors, and like to stop for a consultation with the reflections in a store window while walking. They look at themselves so often, and so intensely, that they're usually well-turned out.

They know how to maximize their natural beauty and grace, even if it's at the expense of their humility. Solars have so much concern for their own appearance, and for the look of things in general, that as a type they may come to rely on appearances to an unfortunate degree.

A Solar wants to latch onto simple solutions, even for those problems where the simple won't suffice. If he's presented with a belief spelled out in a few syllables, he's tempted to catch hold of it and never think that he's missed something hidden, or worry about its implications. Complicated arguments are confusing and cloud his mood, and he doesn't care for the shadow they throw over him. He'll bunch his brows if you present him with a knotty problem, and work himself into a gloomy lassitude.

Luckily this mood won't hold him long. You may see a Solar deep in a funk, but he's easily revived, and his sense of play can break through almost any dark moment. Then he rises, ready for an escapade, and once again his eyes sparkle and his cheeks are flushed. Cares are forgotten with the promise of adventure, and clouds are swept away by another feverish round of activity. Soon he's spinning through the room from friend to friend, showering everyone with his radiance, and for a few moments he dazzles our more ordinary eyes with his unearthly and beautiful light, and then he's gone.

GODS AND

PLANETS

WHEN WERE THE PLANETS NAMED for the chief gods of the most ancient religions? Although this notable date has been lost in time, their names have been linked since the dawn of civilization. We know that while the study of astronomy was becoming more specialized, it was also being wedded to religion.

These early religions, in turn, gave birth to various mythologies that fired some of the first, and some of the greatest, of our ancestors' exploits in literature, science, philosophy, art, and education. The gods and goddesses, whose actions had long been called on to explain an enigmatic world, were eventually joined to the planets, and planet and god became one.

Body types connects these gods and their planets with human types, and with the glands of the endocrine system. By doing so it has given us a new angle on some very old knowledge. The merging of antique gods and medieval alchemy with modern astronomy and endocrinology provides us with an entirely new way to scrutinize man.

In the study of body types this scrutiny progresses in two fields, from two points of view. We see each endocrine gland as the author of a particular group of functions, and also as one participant in a complete system of functions. We study the gods and goddesses similarly, trying to extract from our observations an idea of the unique function each personifies in human activity, while also trying to determine the position each god and goddess occupies in the pantheon of the gods. These parallels continue in the study of the solar system, where individual planets vary to a great degree, yet form a cohesive whole, complete and harmonious.

From the mosaic that's built up by these observations we plot the coordinates that connect not just the glands, gods, and planets, but that indicate the shape of men as well. The weave in which these studies are combined is reminiscent of the pattern of human society. Although we can look for correspondences among these very different worlds, we can't expect a simple and symmetric picture to come from glands, gods, or planets any more than we can expect it from our uncles, friends, or peers.

*   *   *

The planets we relate to body types are the sun, the moon, Mercury, Venus, Mars, Jupiter, and Saturn. These are the objects that have always been visible in our skies. They dominate our myths, and have given their names to the human types. They themselves exist within the whirling phenomena of the astronomical universe.

When we try to describe the universe we run into a peculiar problem: we're unable to comprehend the numbers used to describe it. For instance, the universe is supposed to be about 13 billion (13,000,000,000) years old. Now try to imagine the age it may eventually attain. Stretches that are measured in billions of years don't describe to me a length of time; they tell me about our inability to comprehend them. Their immensity removes them from the scope of our understanding.

The catalog of facts and processes we don't understand swells as quickly as our knowledge increases. We can add to it the form and the size of the universe itself, the way it was born, and whether it will die. As the universe expands, which it seems to be doing, perhaps every piece of "space" and every location in "time" stretch as well, changing imperceptibly the very weave of "reality". Even when we attempt to study the individuals that populate the universe—the largest of which are galaxies—we're left just as puzzled by our knowledge.

Galaxies are the citizens of the visible and energetic universe. Astronomers have estimated their number at 100 billion individuals, each containing billions of stars. These amalgams of dust, gas and stars are held together by their own gravitational force, and are simultaneously being pulled apart by the force of their spin as they rotate through space.

We don't know how galaxies relate to the universe as

a whole, or whether they all revolve around the same center. We see them gathered into clusters in which the individual galaxies are still distinct. A "typical" galaxy is a disc about 100,000 light years in diameter. This means that the flash of a star at one end of the disc, travelling at the speed of light (186,000 miles per second), would take a thousand centuries to reach the other side of its galaxy.

Within the 100 billion stars that constitute the *Milky Way*—our galaxy—our sun lies some 30,000 light years from the galaxy's center; it takes 200 million years to complete one orbit around the galactic core.

The star that animates our family of planets may be 4,560 million years old. During that time the sun somehow created or captured the planets that have evolved into a coherent system of satellites, and which still circle it. While astronomers and physicists have learned a great deal about the evolution of stars, the forces responsible for it remain obscure. We can't see far enough or well enough to study the laws and principles involved in this process; they're simply beyond our reach.

Our sun, like all stars, generates energy and power at hellish heats and crushing pressures, conditions that lie well beyond our imagination and alien to our understanding. Nevertheless, men have connected the light and heat generated by our star with its evolution, and perhaps for that reason have seen in the sun the embodiment of our own highest functions: thought, awareness, and love.

*   *   *

The sun is an astounding creation. It's a huge gaseous globe more than 100 times the size of the Earth. It has more than a million times the volume of the Earth, more than 330,000 times the mass, but it's only one-quarter as dense. The sun's fiery core reaches temperatures of up to 20 million degrees centigrade. It also contains every element found on Earth. Virtually all of the mass of its entire system of planets, asteroids, satellites, comets, dust clouds and random debris, in fact, is contained within the brilliant ball of the sun.

The sun has usually been called Sol, and may have been known at an earlier time as Uranus. Occasionally the Greeks called it Hyperion, but to them it was most of all Apollo, the sun-god.

Like many of the other Greek gods and their Roman descendants, Apollo doesn't seem to play a role in the scheme of types. But the cultural and religious qualities of other ancient gods parallel the qualities of the planets that bear their names. And the gods and planets taken together possess uncanny similarities to their namesakes among the planetary types.

*   *   *

Selene drove the chariot that carried the moon across the sky; she was goddess of the moon for the ancient Greeks. The Romans called her Luna. She is often mentioned with Artemis, a primitive goddess who protected women, brought fertility to the farms of the people, and ruled uncultivated land and forests.

Artemis was known as a "lion unto women"; she was a virgin, the goddess of birth, and she slew the hunter Orion. She was the daughter of Zeus and Apollo's sister. Artemis was also a huntress; she's often shown in sculptures and paintings draped with the skins of her prey.

In a later age we find the attributes of Artemis being appropriated by Diana, an ancient Italian deity of the woods, of women, and of fertility. Diana originally lacked a clear connection to the moon, but the passage of time blended Selene, Luna, Artemis and Diana into one image. Today it's Diana that comes to mind when we think of the huntress who is goddess of the silvery orb of the moon. Diana was both moody and persistent. In these two traits she resembles the Earth's satellite, which passes through moody phases, but which also accompanies us as our regular and constant companion.

The Earth and Moon have sometimes been called a "double planet." Compared to the other moons in our solar system, ours is certainly closer and more nearly equal in size to the Earth than any of the other moons are to the planets that they circle.

The moon's size and distance are such that a precise, mathematical coincidence of the strangest variety takes place each time it moves into alignment between the Earth and the sun. To observers on Earth during these alignments, called solar eclipses, the disc of the moon appears to be exactly the size of the disc of the sun.

Consequently, as the moon swings in front of the sun, it blots it out completely.

While even the largest satellites of Jupiter and Saturn are nowhere near as large as their hosts, our moon is much closer to the size, density, and volume of the Earth. For instance, the moon is about one-quarter the size of the Earth. Jupiter's Ganymede, one of the largest moons in the solar system, is barely a thirtieth the size of its host.

Our moon travels through an elliptical orbit 240,000 miles away from us. It has become so dependent on the Earth that its revolution has come to equal its own rotation. Because of these identical movements, as the moon wheels and spins through our skies, it shows only one side of itself to us on the Earth.

Although the moon retains its aura of mystery by remaining eternally half-hidden, it influences us throughout its phases. Its gravity pulls and releases us as it waxes and wanes, just as it pulls and releases the oceans, creating spring and neap tides each month. The moon seems to act on the human body, which is almost as watery as the oceans. It echoes women's menstrual cycles, and each month it reputedly drives many people to lunatic or violent actions.

The moon may have an iron core, but it has a weak magnetic field, no atmosphere, and no weather. Because it lacks the protection of a gaseous atmosphere, it offers no resistance to the dust, debris, and passing protons and electrons of the solar wind that bombard it. No water flows on the moon, and no forms of life grow there.

Some see in the moon a child of Earth; some, Earth's captive. But it's our steadfast attendant, and, in many of its movements, predictable. Because it reflects so much of the sun's light the Romans associated it with Jupiter, their early sky-god, who they worshipped during the full moon. The brightness of the full moon, added to that of the sun, made for that time of the month when there was the most light from the sky.

The moon's unearthly chill has always implied to men the secret whispers of our own dark thoughts. It seems to advocate hidden schemes, to promote madness, and to champion shadowy sleep like that of Endymion, Selene's lover. The moon's intimate relationship to the Earth's magnetic and gravitational fields makes it our partner. Perhaps it collects the energy the Earth scatters into space; perhaps it passes its own influence back to us by a method we haven't yet observed. But the Earth and the moon are definitely bound in some special, unique relation.

*   *   *

As he had with Artemis, Zeus makes another contribution to the pantheon of gods with Aphrodite, his daughter. She was honored for hundreds of years as the goddess of beauty, fertility, and love. She was raised from the sea, loved the warrior Ares, and bore Aeneas after copulating with Anchises, a mortal. She championed Anchises' tribe, the Trojans, and took their side in their epic war with the Athenians, as recounted by Homer.

Aphrodite was sexuality, and she was love. On occasion prostitutes could be hired in her temples—perhaps due to an overly literal translation of her role in the arts of love. The myrtle was sacred to Aphrodite, as was the dove. She was the goddess of the sea, which had borne her, and by extension, the goddess of sailors. Aphrodite's honors were absorbed by Venus who had been, until that time, an obscure Italian goddess of vegetable nature and fertility.

Artists throughout history have found in Venus' often blatant sexuality, and in the wars of love she waged with Mars, some of their favorite subjects. Poets have seen in her sexuality a sign of creative and procreative powers, and likened it to a cosmic force that pervades nature. She is represented by the planet that is nearer to us than any other, the brightest planet in our sky, the planet that is the most similar to the Earth.

Venus, perfectly round and white, is closer to the sun than any planet except Mercury, and has the most circular orbit of all the planets. The Chinese called it *Tai-pe*, "beautiful white one." To the Babylonians it was *Ishtar*, "bright torch of heaven." Venus' soft, pearly appearance is produced by the sunlight that reflects off the dense layers of cloud that cover it and veil it from the Earth.

At one time Venus may have had oceans. If it did, they were boiled off as the sun gradually grew hotter, steaming the planet and creating what is now a kind of super greenhouse. The atmosphere, over 50 miles of haze on top of clouds on top of haze, covers a planet where the "air" presses ninety times as hard as the Earth's does. Its surface is strewn with rocks, boulders and shale-like stones. Although Venus' density is almost identical to the Earth's, its magnetic field, which is like the electromagnetic signature of a planet, is very weak.

Time on Venus is peculiar, but not because of its year; it takes about 225 of our days for Venus to circle the sun, while it takes the Earth 365 days. But its rotation, which accounts for day and night on the surface of the planet, is very slow.

Drifting along, actually rotating in the opposite direction to the other planets, Venus takes over 20 of our days to sprint once through a complete spin. In other words, an hour on Venus lasts about two of its own weeks; each minute is a quarter of a day.

Venus is very slow, and very hot, and is bathed in a great deal more of the sun's radiation than we are. Beautiful and serene, it hides its late hour pursuits. Venus is never observable the whole night, losing itself in the angles of our respective orbits. In many ways it remains a languorous, lovely, and indistinct mystery.

*   *   *

The phallus was the characteristic emblem of Hermes, one of the youngest of the Olympians. While his primitive origins are flaunted by this emblem of fertility, his cunning is evident everywhere. On the first day of his life, Hermes invented the lyre, robbed his brother Apollo, and then was reconciled with him; a quick study. He was the messenger for the gods, especially for Zeus, his father, and he carried their symbol on his errands, the caduceus of bound rods.

Hermes was widely known in the ancient world by primitive stone columns, called herms, which featured a young man's curly-haired head carved at the top, sometimes with a winged hat set on his head, and sometimes, sticking out half-way down the column, an enormous, erect penis.

Mercurius, the Roman god of traders and those who travelled the roads, became associated with Hermes the messenger, and gathered his traits as well. He became the god of thieves, the god of the oratorical arts, and the god of athletic young men. He was also the patron of literature. We see Hermes' most mysterious role when he serves as attendant and guide to the souls he accompanies on their journey after death. In this capacity he carries the magic wand of the necromancer.

Mercury had little interest in morals or philosophy, and almost none in civic responsibility. His concerns revolved around himself. He had the same amoral isolation as a child enclosed within his own world. Perhaps it was the elusive quickness of the messenger, the same quickness that flashes through the Mercurial type, that allied him to the swiftest planet.

Mercury's closeness to the sun makes it seem like a child tagging behind its parent in the sky, and also

makes it difficult to observe because we're usually looking at it against the backdrop of the sun's glare. It moves
across the ball of the sun only in its crescent phase,
when it's no more than a sliver. It passes behind the sun
when it's full, and very close to the sun when it's in front
and observable. We can't ever see Mercury clearly,
against a wholly dark background, and can only observe
it in fleeting moments. Even then it's obscured.

The heavily cratered surface of Mercury is constantly bombarded not only by solar radiation, but by
the intensity of the solar wind. With no atmosphere, its
temperatures are extreme, ranging from 90 to 600
degrees Kelvin. Most of Mercury's magnetic field is
thought to have been blown away by the intense radiation of the sun. Now it's only about one-hundredth as
strong as the magnetic field of the Earth.

A third the size of Earth, but with 95% less mass,
Mercury revolves around the sun in a year that lasts
only 88 earth days. Its orbit is the most eccentric in the
solar system except for Pluto. Both the evolution and
the inner composition of the planet remain a mystery.
Mercury is so difficult to observe that we'll have to wait
for further exploration to penetrate the riddles of this
hot, erratic and arid sphere.

*   *   *

One of the strangest and most perverse tales in
mythology is the history of the world's beginnings and
the rise of the gods that's recounted by the Greeks. In

135

this story Kronos, youngest son of Heaven and Earth and leader of his fellow gods, the Titans, castrates his father on his mother's advice; she wanted to prevent him from producing any more competition.

Kronos marries his sister Titan, Rhea, and sires what were to become the Olympian gods: Hestia; Demeter, the most important figure in the Eleusinian Mysteries; Hera, Olympian queen; Hades, God of the underworld; Poseidon, ocean ruler; and Zeus.

Kronos, still ridding himself of unwanted competition, did nothing to hurt his vicious reputation by eating all these children except Zeus, who was smuggled out of harm's reach by his mother. Rhea then managed to get Kronos to regurgitate her other children who, led by Zeus, went on to conquer their father and preside over both heaven and earth from their home on Mount Olympus.

This story of warring gods and the cosmic events surrounding Kronos melted into the attributes of the Roman Saturnus, god of harvests, who also had the merriest festival of the year dedicated to him each December.

Saturnus governed seeds and their sowing, and after the fall of the Titans, came down to Italy to teach the natives agriculture, and thereby to civilize them. In joining the unpleasant Kronos with their own ancient god Saturnus, the Latin myth makers captured the grandest aspects of both, and it is the grandest planet of our solar system that bears his name.

Saturn, almost ten times as far from the sun as the

Earth, is the last of the inner planets, and stands on the edge of the immense distances that stretch further out from the center of the solar system to Uranus, Neptune and Pluto. Second in size only to Jupiter, it passes through, and may be affected by, the long tail of Jupiter's vast magnetic field. Its mass, also second only to Jupiter's, is almost a hundred times the Earth's, and it is voluminous enough to contain more than seven hundred Earths.

A great gaseous giant, Saturn seems to be composed principally of hydrogen and helium, as is Jupiter, but in a different mixture. Its atmosphere is topped by a muted haze that covers multi-colored layers of methane, ammonia, and sulphur clouds. It spins amazingly fast, and its day only lasts a little over 10 hours. But the grandest aspect of Saturn, its true insignia, is the incredible system of rings of frozen ice and rock that orbits along with the planet and reaches 50,000 miles beyond the cloud tops of Saturn's muggy atmosphere.

The rings of Saturn have taught astronomers a great deal about the planet's satellites. We know of more than 20 satellites circling Saturn, the biggest array supported by any planet. Most of them are nothing more than frozen rocks. Titan, the largest, is the only moon in the solar system with its own atmosphere. From the evidence of the rings, and from periodic radio emissions that it produces, astronomers have deduced that some evolutionary process may be occurring on Saturn. These radio emissions take place with an odd, metronomic regularity, a radio-electric pulse once a day, at noon—Saturn time.

Saturn also has a massive magnetic field, 1,000 times larger than Earth's, which may be the offshoot of an unobserved energy cycle. Maybe some of these familiar planets will someday become suns themselves, roaring through the galaxy with their own planetary systems. It's easy to picture the majestic, immense Saturn as one of these nascent suns.

*   *   *

Yet another branch of the tree of Zeus is Ares, the Greek warrior god. He was an unlovely god who, like Hermes, had no essential moral functions. To the ancients Ares didn't stand simply for war, which they waged to conquer territory or to defend their homes. What they saw in him was everything bloody and brutal that went with war.

It was Ares who instigated vicious acts, who fell into tempestuous loves, who sired ferocious, violent and outrageous sons, and who supported foreign foes like the Trojans, or unusually warlike ones like the Amazons. Aphrodite was his common companion and the mother of two of his children. He had no concern for right or wrong on the battlefield, and even to those who worshipped him, he was an unpopular god.

Ferocious in aspect, courageous in action, Ares easily became associated with one of the oldest Italian gods, Mars, whose power was second only to Jupiter's.

His primitive nature encompassed the fields of agriculture and the fields of war, on both of which he strove to protect the native lands.

The wolf, who gave succor to his son Romulus, is sacred to Mars, as is the woodpecker. Many festivals and competitions were held in his honor in Rome, and he also became the god of the state as the empire became more military.

The planet Mars is his worthy namesake. To us Mars is red in the night sky; we call it the *angry* planet. In this angry aspect of Mars, and in his inflamed and florid features, we recognize his planet.

Mars is the first planet beyond the orbit of the Earth, and appears brighter than all others except Venus, his consort, who lies between the Earth and the sun. Mars travels an orbit so eccentric and extreme that, during its closest approach to the sun, the heat it receives varies by as much as 40 percent. Its distance from the sun varies as well, getting as much as twenty percent closer or farther away during a year that lasts 20 of our months.

Mars is about a third the size of the Earth. It is the least dense of the planets, and has a weak magnetic field more like the moon's. Its thin atmosphere, dominated by carbon dioxide, stretches over a chaotic terrain of sand dunes and icy rocks, canyons ten times the size of the Grand Canyon, and gigantic volcanoes 16 miles tall. Dense clouds whip themselves into cyclones in this hostile environment, volcanoes erupt, and landslides thunder through the mountains. Occasionally the most impressive storms in the solar system blow up on Mars, sending furious clouds of dust sweeping over the planet, and darkening it for months.

The obvious change of seasons on Mars, the markings that look like channels, and its proximity to the Earth have regularly excited the minds of observers, but it displays no evidence of life. Its only moons are two odd, misshapen rocks that have no more sign of life on their surface than Mars does. They are named for Phobos and Deimos, who were the war god's children and his charioteers; their names mean fear and rout.

*   *   *

In agricultural societies, man's difficulties as well as the bounty of his harvests seemed to come to him through the agency of the sky and its weather. In primitive religions the sky itself is usually reserved as an attribute for the most potent god of the pantheon. For the Greeks, Zeus combined all their ancient sky-gods with the warrior who had defeated and imprisoned Kronos and the other Titans, bringing to Earth a new reign. Zeus in turn was credited with siring a host of the most important Olympians: Athena, Artemis, Apollo, Ares, and Dionysus among them. His loves were many, and his incestuous marriage to his sister Hera was sometimes stormy.

After the battle to overthrow the Titans, retold fantastically by Hesiod, the rule of the world was divided in three; Zeus's brothers Hades and Poseidon ruled over

Hell and the seas, while Zeus himself held sway over heaven and earth. Zeus is an ancient fertility god who copulated with goddesses, nymphs and mortals, spawning characters that criss-cross the convoluted and inbred world of Greek mythology. He guarded the family, and was worshipped in connection with almost every side of Greek life.

Zeus ruled by might rather than by righteousness over a squabbling fraternity of gods and goddesses. Even so, he is the protector of the laws and of the king and, despite his harsh character, he also guards political freedom and public morals. Zeus could erupt as Thunderous Zeus when he rewarded the good or punished the evil. The stoic philosophers recognized in Zeus the principle of fiery reason, which they took to be the highest in the universe, and which they thought pervaded and animated all of creation.

When the Greek gods were woven into the Roman pantheon, Zeus was naturally transformed into Jupiter, an old Italian sky god. The Romans worshipped Jupiter at the full moon, and made him responsible for weather and thunderstorms. Jupiter presided at the triumphs of generals and protected treaties and oaths. He was the son and conqueror of Saturn, cager of the Titans, and sire of the Roman equivalent of Zeus' children. The worship of Jupiter developed into a glittery cult with many festivals and rites. It's fitting that the greatest of gods is symbolized by the fifth planet, the tremendous gaseous giant of Jupiter.

Next to the ringed glory of Saturn, Jupiter is the

141

most visually startling planet. It's a multicolored ball of flowing winds and gas that roil its atmosphere of hydrogen, helium, methane, ammonia gas, and ammonia crystals. Unknown forces on Jupiter have created incredible atmospheric effects, among them an oval spot some 30,000 miles long, and bright red. Composed primarily of liquids, Jupiter spins so fast that its gaseous globe has flattened somewhat at the poles and bulged at the equator. It completes a rotation about once every 10 hours.

The development of Jupiter has somehow made it by far the most massive planet in the Solar System. Two-thirds of all the mass of all the planets, their moons, rings, and dust, belongs to Jupiter; it's well over 300 times as massive as the Earth.

Jupiter is surrounded by at least 16 satellites as well as a faint system of rings. One of these satellites, Ganymede, is the solar system's largest moon; it's slightly larger than the planet Mercury. The four largest Jovian moons are so huge that Galileo was able to discover them using only his seventeenth-century instruments. Heavily-cratered Callisto and strangely reflective Europa are also large, but Jupiter has the most interesting relationship with the closest of the four, the enigmatic Io.

Jupiter produces the largest, most powerful magnetic field of all the planets. It manufactures energy in a process that seems to be speeding up as Jupiter becomes less and less dense. It throws off intense, fluctuating radio signals, and has created what is in effect an enormous dynamo, with Io as a moving part. Jupiter appears to some astronomers to be connected to Io by a "tube" of electrical energy that pulses with seventy times the generating capacity of all the power-plants on Earth.

Whether this mechanism controls, escalates, or regulates Jupiter's complex magnetic field and huge radiation belts is uncertain, but it may affect the electromagnetic radiation produced by the planet. The radio signals it produces last anywhere from a few minutes to several hours. These signals sometimes indicate that bursts of cosmic rays and trapped particles are being flung from Jupiter's magnetic field so forcefully that they're travelling at close to the speed of light.

The most fascinating coincidence in the analogy between planets and people is connected to these Jovian forces, and to the changes they are working over enormous spans of time. These changes, which seem to reveal Jupiter as a planet that's on its way to becoming a star, are parallel to drastic changes that may occur for men as well.

It's at Jupiter's position on the enneagram that the flow of types, which has been endlessly coursing through their fixed points, can jump to a new level. At this point Jupiter's evolution from planet to star becomes an image representative of human evolution. It's an image that suggests a possibility for man that's as new and as radical as Jupiter's transformation; the possibility that a man could become a self-generating, illuminating, and energizing individual. That he could become a man who is himself poised, like Jupiter, on the threshold of a transcendental rebirth.

GLANDS AND

BEHAVIOR

EXTENDING THROUGHOUT the human body is a network of specialized glands that controls much of our behavior by sending hormones—minute amounts of chemicals—as messengers into our blood. They are called the *endocrine*, or ductless, glands, and they regulate many of our basic physiological processes: metabolism, growth, reproduction, and the maintenance of the body's internal environment. Our survival, both as individuals and as a species, depends on these glands' proper activity and healthy functioning.

The endocrine system is composed of a pituitary, with both a posterior and an anterior part, hypothalamus, thyroid, parathyroid, adrenal cortex and adrenal medulla, islands of Langerhans in the pancreas, female ovaries and male testes, the placenta in pregnant women, and the pineal body, which is lodged in the brain a small distance behind the hypothalamus. The glands vary in size and, taken together, form a complex mechanism in which their effects often contradict each another. The opposition inherent in their work enables them to balance many of the body's functions.

The endocrine glands also play a special part in the theory of body types, one deeply rooted in history. In this theory, some of the correspondences invented by the medieval alchemists have been borrowed, modified, and then applied to the endocrine glands. The result is that each of these glands is presumed to receive the influences of the planet with which it is associated.

Today's medical science still lacks a complete knowledge of the endocrine glands. Although researchers can observe them more critically, and measure their functions more precisely than ever, they have only succeeded in producing new questions rather than definite answers. Even some of the functions of the glands remain a mystery.

The endocrine glands keep a constant watch over the levels of different hormones in the blood as they circulate, in turn, through each gland. When a gland senses an imbalance in the hormones for which it is responsible, it reacts.

The action the gland will take is usually to issue a hormone of its own into the bloodstream, calling on the body to produce a substance that will correct the imbalance. Endocrine cells produce hormones which are carried in blood to target cells. These hormones not only carry the gland's message, they are themselves the message, and they find the cells their message is intended for in an ingenious way.

Like a key cut to fit the path of a lock, each of these

Globe Press Books
P.O. Box 2045
Madison Square Station
New York, NY 10159

Thank You for purchasing this book from Globe Press Books. We are very interested in your reactions, thoughts, and comments. Please use this card to let us hear from you. Sending in the card will also keep you informed of new books we are readying for publication. ***Send it today!***

Name: _____

Address: _____

Your Comments: _____

_____

_____

_____

_____

cells is designed to "dock" with a target cell that is constructed to be the exact mate of the message cell. Through this marvelous bit of chemical engineering the endocrine glands quicken, retard, and maintain the enzyme activity in the target cells. It's easy to see why it's said that all body functions can ultimately be reduced to cellular functions.

Our bodies contain about 30 trillion cells. To get an idea of the variety in this tremendous number of the cells that make up our body, look at your arm. Try to imagine a square drawn on your skin, one inch on a side.

If your eyes were acute enough to survey the cells in this plot of ordinary, comfortable, and familiar real estate, they would reveal the following inventory: 500 sweat glands, over 1,000 nerve endings, yards of blood vessels, almost 100 oil glands, 150 sensors to register pressure, heat and cold, and millions of cells. The drop of blood you spilled when you slipped with your letter opener is populated with as many as 5 million red blood cells.

Cells are the smallest individuals in our body. They are capable of reproducing themselves, and of passing along the complex codes and ciphers that determine the genetic inheritance of each of us. They form the smallest building blocks of the body, massing together into tissues, and taking on the life of the tissues they have become. Cells come in quite an assortment of sizes. The largest is the ovum, or egg, produced by menstruating women, which is one twenty-fifth of an inch. The smallest cells are only one thousandth that size.

The endocrine glands constantly measure the ingredients in the blood, and in the fluid between the cells, in order to carry out their essential functions. Some regulate the metabolism of food, fuel, and the availability to the body of other necessary ingredients. Some determine our body's rate of growth and development. Others determine our sexual rhythms, and affect the specialized chemistry and functions of reproduction. Endocrine secretions also control the body's electrical balance, its temperature, and the rate at which it burns energy.

The glands somehow manage to execute all their contrasting and complex responsibilities with exceptional accuracy. They do it amidst changes taking place at every moment, as we pass from one state of mind to another, from attentive study, to surprise, to chagrin. Because our chemical make-up changes in response to each moment's constantly changing conditions, the hormone levels in our bodies vary continually. At every moment survival depends on the endocrine system making precise readings of stimuli and situations, and making appropriate responses.

How do the endocrine glands manage it? They affect all of the body's systems, each of which can be looked at as a group of related functions. The endocrine system itself influences the skeletal, muscular, circulatory, digestive, respiratory, urinary, and reproductive systems. It's controlled, in turn, by the nervous

148

system. In other words, the glands are managed by the brain and its complex extensions—they are one of the vehicles used by the nervous system to keep us alive.

Our nervous system decides when we will act, and when we will react; it's our ruling faculty. It gives rise to primitive rage, and to religious ecstasy. Of its millions of nerve cells—or neurons—half collect information from throughout the body. These neurons concentrate in our sense organs, where they've become specialized, and gather in our spinal cord, along which they relay their information by minute electrical and chemical signals to the other half—the compact mass of the brain.

The language the nervous system speaks is electrochemical, but we haven't mastered its vocabulary. Highway signs, today's breakfast, and the whispers of love all become chemical signals, which are somehow converted into electricity, and back into chemical replies. We have no way of explaining the way that a neuron produces the electrical charge that leaps across space to another, outreaching neuron. Nor can we explain the translation of a physical language of shunting chemicals into what could be considered a metaphysical one, the language of invisible electric charges.

We can, however, trace the effects not only of our intellect, but of the more primitive, subconscious functions we share with other animals. We can follow the flow of these chemical signals along their pathways to their terminals in muscles and glands. We can watch the formation of a response.

These transactions are performed by peripheral

nerves, among which are the autonomic nerves, a subsidiary system that has its own site within the brain where its decisions are made. The autonomic nervous system receives and transmits messages that regulate the iris, and the muscles of the heart, the lungs, the stomach, and the glands.

Lying deep in the brain, between the midbrain and the cerebrum, and just below the thalamus, is the hypothalamus. It is the hypothalamus, the agent of the autonomic nervous system, that relays impulses along the chain of neurons in the spinal cord, and moves them to muscles and glands all over the body. This control of many of our organs, of heartbeat, respiration, the opening and closing of blood vessels and the tightening of the stomach and intestines, is its direct effect, but not its only one.

The nerve cells of the hypothalamus also produce hormones, which they introduce into the body through the posterior part of the pituitary. This little-known gland has no actual secretions of its own, but still seems to play a unique role in the endocrine cycle.

Usually the endocrine glands secrete the hormones which they produce. But the posterior pituitary, which releases the hormones that are created in the hypothalamus, doesn't appear to create any hormones of its own. However, because it is connected to the hypothalamus by its stem, the posterior pituitary seems to connect the world of the glands to the more rarefied world of the brain.

The hypothalamus also sends hormones directly

into the blood through the network of nerves that links the brain and the spinal cord. Via this roundabout route it controls the activity of the anterior pituitary, which in turn affects the activity of many of the other endocrine glands, and rules the internal balance of the human body.

We begin our tour of the endocrine glands in the pancreas, the gland associated with the Lunar body type. The pancreas is important to the process of digestion, and has some small connection to the lymphatic system. It owes its inclusion as an endocrine gland to its clumps of hormone-producing cells known as the islands of Langerhans. Although bits of cellular activity account for only a very small percentage of all the cells in the pancreas, they produce several important hormones.

Insulin, one of the hormones produced by the islands of Langerhans, lowers the level of sugar in the blood. Glucagon, another, raises it. These opposite effects are produced, in the first instance, by stimulating the liver to produce more glucose. In the second, they're produced by increasing the rate at which energy is burned in the cells, effectively reducing the overall glucose level.

The islands of Langerhans also manufacture somatostatin, which is found in many other areas of the body as well. This hormone affects the movement of nutrients from the digestive system into the circulation, and may slow the body's absorbtion of those nutrients.

These associations of the Lunar type with the maintenance of burnable fuel in the carbohydrate chain aren't usually mentioned in the theory of body types. Instead, Lunar is seen as a "watery" type because of the pancreas' connection to the lymphatic system. This system carries essential nutrients, acquired from the digestion of food, to the blood in our veins. The blood then distributes the nutrients to cells throughout the body.

An abundance of lymph is said to be responsible for the Lunar's round and limpid appearance. However, if there is a connection between the pancreas and the lymphatic system, it remains largely unknown to contemporary endocrinology. An explanation has not yet been found for this apparent contradiction, in which the pancreas, and by extension the passive, inert Lunar type, is firmly connected to the cycle of energy production.

Venus is associated with the parathyroids. Actually four small glands that weigh about an ounce each, they sit on the corners of the thyroid gland. The parathyroids produce parathormone (PTH) which opposes and balances calcitonin, a hormone produced by the thyroid. PTH increases the rate at which calcium and phosphorus are transferred from the bones into the bloodstream. It also acts to retain more calcium in the kidneys and digestive system as a whole, which is then passed into the bloodstream.

This balance of calcium is critical to us; it allows the impulses coming from our nerves to move our muscles. The secretion of PTH is controlled by the parathyroids, which monitor the blood, constantly measuring its level of calcium. A lack of calcium produces dire symptoms that are the opposite of the lethargic Venusian body type's habits; muscle spasms, over-excitability, and nervousness that can bring a person close to death.

Over-activity of the parathyroids produces too much calcium and may eventually soften and deform the bones; it also causes calcium and water to be lost in our urine. These actions of the parathyroids on calcium levels in the blood, and their effects, don't necessarily reinforce the picture we have of the earthy, sluggish Venusian type. Perhaps more knowledge is yet to be uncovered about this vital gland and its essential work.

The thyroid, about an ounce of tissue in two lobes joined by an isthmus, straddles the windpipe; it is the gland of Mercury. It is roused to activity by the hypothalamus and the anterior pituitary. One of its hormones—calcitonin—lowers the calcium level of the blood, and works in opposition to the parathyroids. But another of its secretions, called the thyroid hormone, affects us in more wide-ranging, and more dramatic, ways.

The thyroid hormone exerts its authority by controlling the activity of enzymes, which in turn control the speed at which energy is consumed in the cells of the body. Through this control it affects all the body's processes that require the combustion of energy, including growth. Its effects are monitored in the bloodstream, and provide the hypothalamus and the anterior pituitary with a constant flow of information regarding this crucial bodily process.

153

The messages shuttling from hypothalamus to anterior pituitary to thyroid and back again constitute a feedback mechanism that helps to regulate the amount of heat produced in our bodies, their cholesterol level, heart rate, respiration and blood pressure. The thyroid hormone acts as a catalyst for all these activities by escalating the burning of cellular energy.

A person whose thyroid is over-active becomes nervous, excitable, irritable and apprehensive; traits that are apparent in the Mercurial type. In extreme cases it also causes muscular tremors. Under-activity of the thyroid, on the other hand, makes people lethargic, cools the body, and starves the cells of energy. Because of these wide-ranging effects, the balanced operation of the thyroid is essential to human activity.

In this scheme of endocrine types Saturn is ruled by the anterior pituitary; the so-called *master gland*. It develops from the same tissues, and alongside, the other half of the gland, the posterior pituitary. Dominating several of the other glands, the anterior pituitary is of primary importance in the endocrine system.

The anterior pituitary directly stimulates the thyroid, adrenals, and ovaries; indirectly, it regulates growth, accelerates digestion, and colors the skin. It is located at the base of the brain, in front of—anterior to—the posterior pituitary, through which it is connected to the hypothalamus.

Its own hormones contribute to the production of estrogen and progesterone, the sex hormones of the reproductive system. Although it is tied to Saturn, the

154

most masculine body type, it seems to have at least as many maternal qualities as the posterior part, which is connected to Jovial. One of its hormones, prolactin, helps women's breasts develop when pregnant, and also helps them give milk when nursing.

Over-activity of the anterior pituitary in childhood enlarges people into giants; under-activity of the gland creates dwarfs. In adults an oversupply of some of its hormones stretches the growth of the body's long bones, and creates a condition known as acromegaly.

Mars is linked to the adrenals, a pair of glands atop the kidneys which rules almost as many of our functions as the anterior pituitary does. Divided into two distinct spheres, the adrenals react in complex ways to stimuli from many different sources. Together they spawn more than 30 hormones which affect both the levels of sodium and potassium in the kidneys, and the levels of fats and proteins in the liver. Some adrenal hormones modify the burning of carbohydrates. Others, like the sex hormones oestrogen and androgen, influence the reproductive system.

The adrenal cortex is the outer portion of the adrenals. Adrenal steroids produced here are called on by the anterior pituitary and the hypothalamus, which are constantly monitoring the level of corticosteroids in the blood. A change in this level causes the anterior pituitary to release hormones that in turn stimulate the adrenals to produce other hormones that correct the imbalance.

This is another example of the closed-loop, self-regulating nature of the endocrine system, in which glands communicate and interact with each other through their complimentary chemical sensitivities. This particular process plays a key part in regulating the levels of sodium and potassium, both of which are vital elements in maintaining the electrolytic stability of the body's fluids.

Under-activity of the adrenal cortex, which may allow the level of glucocorticoids in the system to drop, results in Addison's disease. This life-threatening condition weakens the body, causes fatigue, weight loss, and anemia, and intensifies the pigmentation of the skin.

Over-activity is equally devastating, as a lack of potassium can make muscles shake, turn the complexion florid, deprive one of protein, and raise the level of blood sugar. An excess production of glucocorticoids gives rise to Cushing's syndrome, which leads to a thinning of the skin that makes one bruise easily; it can also produce obesity. Over-activity of the adrenal cortex can afflict women with a grotesque virilism in which both male sex characteristics and male secondary sex organs are exaggerated far beyond normal.

The inner part of the adrenals is the medulla which, unlike the cortex, is controlled by the sympathetic nervous system. Through another complex process the adrenal medulla passes its messages to the hypothalamus, and in doing so it bypasses the anterior pituitary. Instead these messages travel through the medulla oblongata, one of the most primitive parts of the brain. One of this gland's chief tasks is to stimulate the manufacture of epinephrine, or adrenaline. The adrenal medulla thus becomes associated with the "fight-or-flight" effects of adrenaline, a hormone that forms an essential part of the nervous system's response to stress.

Strong emotions, a pounding heart, blood flowing through muscles, climbing blood pressure, and the burning of sugar for energy also cause the release of this potent hormone. Adrenaline prolongs the intensity of these functions by many of its effects; it constricts the smooth muscles of the skin, dilates the pupils, tightens the abdominal muscles and blood vessels, supplies more air to the body by relaxing the bronchioles in the windpipe, contracts the sphincter and ureter, mobilizes the fuel in muscles and liver, increases the sugar level and available energy carried by the blood, and generally stimulates our entire metabolism. Adrenaline brings the body and its systems to a head, prepared for immediate, and perhaps extreme, action.

The approach of combat can produce all these physiological changes, and so can the tremble of fear. Both of these reactions are instinctive and automatic; both are necessary for our survival. By catapulting us into violence, or fear, the adrenals demonstrate the very dramatic changes that are brought about by their hormone, adrenaline.

The pituitary gland lies deep in the recesses of the brain, and develops in two distinct directions until, in adults, it becomes a two-lobed gland. In the embryo, the anterior part rises from the roof of the primitive mouth cavity. The posterior part is created from tissue growing up from the floor of the primitive brain, and eventually connects to the adult brain by way of the pituitary stalk.

The posterior pituitary secretes two chief hormones, but produces neither of them. This gland, coupled to the Jovial type, is in one sense an elementary part of the hypothalamus. The hormones the hypothalamus produces are passed to the posterior pituitary for release into the body. One of these hormones has an effect on the fluid balance in the body; the other hormone is oxytocin, which is partly responsible for women's birth contractions, and for the production of milk in nursing mothers.

While our knowledge of the posterior pituitary is very incomplete, the variety of roles it plays makes it fascinating. It acts not only as an endocrine gland, but also as an integral part of the hypothalamus, by releasing the antidiuretic hormone, made in the hypothalamus, into the body.

The antidiuretic hormone performs a crucial service by helping to keep the body's internal environment in balance. This balance, or equilibrium, is called *homeostasis*. It includes the body's temperature, appetite and thirst, its electrolytic balance, and its acid-base balance. It also includes the body's overall level of energy. By bringing balance, or harmony, to the body's homeostasis, the posterior pituitary helps to ensure man's survival.

The thymus, a small gland composed of a mass of white blood cells, is located in the upper chest under the breastbone. It is associated with the Solar type. This

158

gland grows throughout childhood, but starts to shrink after puberty. It produces some hormone-like substances which affect the immune system's development, and it influences the way the immune system functions.

The thymus also processes white blood cells, or lymphocytes, which provide one of the body's basic defenses against foreign invasion. Lymphocytes excite other cells of the immune system to produce the antibodies that the body summons to combat alien infestation and infection. An imbalance in any of this work can rout the body's defenses and make it susceptible to disease.

The sex organs—men's testes and women's ovaries—are related to Uranus, a planet that doesn't represent a specific type in the scheme of body types. Instead, it stands for the creative, and procreative, functions in all men. But the sex organs also direct a part of the endocrine system's control of body functions. These glands produce sex hormones that govern the development of secondary sex organs and secondary sex characteristics. The anterior pituitary and the hypothalamus dominate the work of the testes and the ovaries.

A man's secondary sex organs are those that produce and transport spermatozoa, and include the penis. The hormones that control these organs also determine the quality of his secondary sex characteristics; the deepness of his voice, the amount of his pubic and body hair, and the general shape and character to his body that make it male.

Women's ovaries produce the hormones that chan-

nel the development of their secondary sex organs.
These hormones influence the organs that produce and
deliver the eggs, or ova, to be fertilized, and the vagina.
They spur the changes in a woman's breasts that are
necessary for her to feed her young. Normal breast
development, the amount of a woman's body hair, the
typical proportions and rounded curves of the female
body, are all secondary sex characteristics whose character is dictated by these same hormones.

The last endocrine gland we will look at is the pineal
body. This small cone-shaped gland is buried deep in
the brain, midway between the temples and centered
directly behind the eyes. Body types relates the pineal
gland to Neptune, another planet lacking a connection
to a specific type. Neptune supplies us instead with a
symbol of a higher type of man; one in whom a new
function operates.

Despite a good deal of investigation, the pineal
remains largely unknown. Researchers suspect that it
reacts to the amount of light our eyes take in. They
think that it produces melatonin, a hormone somehow
involved with the menstrual cycle, which may inhibit the
work of the ovaries.

In some lower animals the pineal develops into an
eye-like structure called the pineal eye. Partly because
of this evidence it is sometimes thought to be the rem-
nant of a primitive sense organ. But in many mystic sci-
ences the pineal gland is credited with being the seed
of man's higher functions, those which remain potential
and inactivate in normal life. These functions are

thought to be connected to some *third eye*; a new, rather than a vestigial, sense. What these higher faculties may be, and how the pineal affects them, are questions closed to scientific explanation for the time being.

The work of the pineal gland remains as mysterious as its effects are elusive. It may be, as René Descartes said, the organ of "common sense." But it also hints at the possibility that the body might yet develop new ways to control its higher, more psychic work.

The pineal gland also represents a new possibility for man— his chance to develop new, and higher, psychic functions. What these functions and their effects would be we can only guess, as we can only guess what they would mean for the person who had managed to acquire them.

CONCLUSION

I HOPE THIS BRIEF LOOK at body types has opened a new way for you to study and to understand both yourself and others. Although *Body Types* is far from being a complete investigation of human types, it is the first extended treatment of this idea.

Whether body types initially seem important or not, you may find them popping up at odd moments, or appearing in the typical behavior of people you know. Perhaps you'll notice your own routine actions, and how difficult it is to change them. It's when we see our predictability that we understand how our lives are ruled by type. We get a hint of how widely types can be applied, and what they might mean—there isn't a single human expression that isn't affected by type.

But the study of types also suggests a way out of the routines of thinking, acting, and feeling in which we're so often caught, and that ruin our chances for a more individual life. In fact, the ability of body types to help us create a truly individual existence is their most potent, and most hopeful, achievement.

BIBLIOGRAPHY

Anthony, Catherine Parker and Thibodeau, Gary A. *Structure and Function of the Body*. St. Louis: Times Mirror/Mosby College Publishing, 1984.

Berman, Louis, M.D. *The Glands Regulating Personality*. New York: 1929.

Boardman, John. *The Parthenon and its Sculptures*. Austin: University of Texas Press, 1985.

Bulfinch, Thomas. *Bulfinch's Mythology*. New York: Thomas Y. Crowell Company, n.d.

Clark, Kenneth. *The Nude*. Princeton, New Jersey: Princeton University Press, 1972. Princeton/Bollingen Edition.

Collin, Rodney. *The Theory of Celestial Influence*. New York: Samuel Weiser, Inc., 1971. Fourth Impression.

—— *The Theory of Eternal Life*. Boulder and London: Shambhala, 1984.

The Concise Columbia Encyclopedia. New York: Avon, 1983.

Flaceliere, Robert. *A Literary History of Greece*. Chicago: Aldine Publishing Company, 1964. Trans. by Douglas Garman.

Groenewegen-Frankfort, H.A., and Ashmole, Bernard. *Art of the Ancient World*. New York: Harry N. Abrams, Inc., n.d.

Gurdjieff, George. *Meetings with Remarkable Men*. New York: E.P. Dutton & Company, Inc., 1963.

—— *Views from the Real World*. New York: E.P. Dutton, 1975.

Hammond, N.G.L., and Scullard, H.H., eds. *The Oxford Classical Dictionary.* Oxford: Clarendon Press, 1977. Second Edition.

Hinnells, John R., ed. *The Penguin Dictionary of Religions.* Middlesex, England: Penguin Books, 1984.

Kitto, H.D.F. *The Greeks.* Great Britian: Penguin Books, 1979.

McNaught, Ann B., and Callander, Robin. *Illustrated Physiology.* Edinburgh, London and New York: Churchill Livingstone, 1983. Fourth Edition.

Moore, Patrick, and Hunt, Garry. *Atlas of the Solar System.* Chicago, New York and San Francisco: Rand McNally & Company, 1984.

Ouspensky, P.D. *The Fourth Way.* New York: Vintage Books, 1971.

—— *A New Model of the Universe.* New York: Vintage Books, 1971.

—— *The Psychology of Man's Possible Evolution.* New York: Vintage Books, 1974.

—— *In Search of the Miraculous.* New York and London: Harcourt Brace Jovanovich, 1977.

—— *Tertium Organum.* New York: Alfred A. Knopf, 1968. 3rd American Edition, authorised and revised. Trans. by Nicholas Bessaraboff and Claude Bragdon.

Ovid. *The Metamorphoses.* N.p.: The New American Library, 1964. Trans. by Horace Gregory.

Plutarch. *The Lives of the Noble Grecians and Romans.* New York: The Modern Library, n.d. Trans. by John Dryden. Revised by Arthur Hugh Clough.

Redgrove, H. Stanley. *Alchemy: Ancient and Modern.* New Hyde Park, NY: University Books, 1969. Second Edition.

Reyner, J.H. *The Diary of a Modern Alchemist.* London: Neville Spearman, 1974.

Spence, Lewis. *An Encyclopaedia of Occultism.* New Hyde Park, NY: University Books, 1968.

Stassinopoulos, Arianna, and Beny, Roloff. *The Gods of Greece.* London: Weidenfeld & Nicolson, 1983.

164

INDEX

PUBLISHER'S NOTE

YOU CAN FIND OUT MORE about body types and the other ideas discussed in this book by writing to the publisher at the address below. You will be told how to contact the Fourth Way school in which, using the principles of Gurdjieff, Ouspensky, and others, these ideas are being actualized.

*   *   *

Body Types is the initial publication of Globe Press Books, and the first of three works that are intended to introduce some of the basic ideas of the Fourth Way. The second book will survey the vastly different minds that operate within us, and the third will examine the blindnesses that keep us from accomplishing our aims.

With this program, Globe Press Books continues the tradition of publishing from within a Fourth Way school that was begun by George Gurdjieff and amplified by Peter Ouspensky, Rodney Collin, Maurice Nicoll, and A.R. Orage. *Body Types* is offered in the spirit of this tradition, and with deep gratitude for our predecessors' efforts.

GLOBE PRESS BOOKS

BOX 2045 MADISON SQUARE STATION NEW YORK NY 10159